The Unwrapped Leader

Become a Gifted Leader
In Your Network Marketing Business

Paperback ISBN: 9798839539648
Hardcover ISBN: 9798351795577

A review of "The Unwrapped Leader"...

"Love it.

It has come together well and brings them on a journey.

The "Unwrapped Leader" will bring you on a journey from that first "yes" to uncovering the leader hidden deep within us all just waiting to be discovered. I have often used the analogy that our beautiful profession is a gift just waiting to be unwrapped, and many of us only peak inside without unwrapping the whole gift. This book gives you the insights, tools and skills to unwrap the gift and then unwrap yourself to create the success and life you want, plus, even more importantly, to enjoy the journey as you uncover the person you become along the way. Dracy and Teisha have done a powerful job in presenting this information in an easy-to-read book and I encourage anyone wanting to be successful in their Direct Selling career to take the time, to not only read, but to implement the many nuggets contained within."

— Celine Egan, CEO, Juice Plus (Australia) Pty Ltd

Foreword by Tom Chenault

My name is Tom Chenault and I have the honor of writing the foreword of this book. I am so proud to have been chosen to do it. I have been in the network marketing profession for over 30 years and when I see two people have written a book that will literally advance where this profession is going, I want to be a part of it.

I have been a successful network marketer myself and have spoken on the biggest stages all over the world. I also have the longest running home-based business radio show/podcast on the planet. My latest obsession is changing the way the world views network marketing by teaching and training people to look at people first as human beings they can serve versus just "prospects" with an app, a concept and a community called Contact Mapping.

I had "heard" of Dracy Dewar long before I ever got to meet her. She was bigger than life and I was intimidated when I went to Australia to be around her for a few weeks. You will read about her accomplishments in this book, but know that anything I have done pales in comparison to hers. But after being around her for just thirty minutes I found the real Dracy to be even better. Her mantra is love, collaboration, and communication. She leads with her heart. Her commitment to people is legendary and all she really wants is for everyone to win. She absorbs personal development and network marketing training like a sponge and is a strong enough leader to instill confidence into any person or team.

Teisha is an entirely different story. She is a young woman who got a taste of network marketing in college and found herself in a fantastic quandary. She got a great education and an opportunity to put it to work in a job teaching children. But the network marketing bug had bitten her, and no matter what she tried, she couldn't stop working on that path as well.

This is where this book will set itself apart from the others. As a teacher, Teisha knew she needed one too, a good coach and mentor who had what she wanted. Dracy was a family friend and a legend in the profession. Teisha made the commitment to listen and implement Dracy's teachings. They both documented

2

the process, wins and the losses, to give you a blueprint for building your own business that works for you.

As you read this book, you will see a path that will take you from getting started to having a robust team of your own. With stories and skill training that will prove to you that not only you can do this, but you will see you can teach others to do the same thing. You will see you can build a business based on love, compassion and integrity that has literally everyone you approach, meet, or do business with, feel honored to have met with you instead of that feeling of being sold or played.

This book will have you not only find your "why" — but also live it! People will sense that you are up to something larger than yourself and will want to be a part of it.

Network marketing is hard work that takes a long time to master and succeed in. Any book that shortens that cycle is a good one in my opinion. What you will love about "The Unwrapped Leader" is that Dracy isn't telling you, she is showing you with Teisha. I loved the patience Dracy shows her while still mentoring and I loved Teisha's unwavering willingness to learn. As I read on, I noticed Dracy learning from Teisha too, which is the mark of any great student and leader. As you look at the chapter names you will see they all start with the word "Gift". Which has you wanting to literally unwrap each chapter. The book is challenging and deep but it feels good from the first page on. "The Unwrapped Leader" will give you all you need to launch or further your business in a powerful yet entertaining way. The key will be to learn this book, not just read it. It's one of those.

I read it thinking I was going to know what they said and just validate it. What I found was that there were so many new things to learn that Teisha has mastered along with the fundamentals of network marketing that Dracy embraces so well. It's a gift of this book that you get to experience the wisdom and success of a Dracy Dewar while at the same time getting the fresh perspective of Teisha showing us what is working now, in the age of the internet, social media, and the "new" network marketing.

The more you read this book the more you will understand the magic. That this profession is still the same at its core but enhanced by all the wonderful ideas brought to it by these young, smart, and ambitious people like Teisha.

Read "The Unwrapped Leader" hard and slow. Let it become a part of you like it did for Teisha and long ago for Dracy. Then go change the world like these two women are doing with this book.

Tom Chenault

ContactMapping.com/tom
TheNetworkMarketingLeadershipShow.com

Introduction

Dracy: The Two-Way Street of Coaching & Mentorship

There are two young girls who have been friends for as long as they can remember. Their parents were friends who spent many weekends and holidays together. These girls were always on an adventure — I don't ever remember them playing with dolls or anything like that, but they were always being creative, playing games like Monopoly and LIFE. But what I remember most is their passion for finding ways to make money.

As young as 7 or 8 years old, they had lemonade stands and would buy candy from the local shop and sell it at double the price to the kids in the neighborhood. They even sold their colored drawings. One time, they noticed the local carpet store threw out carpet and tile samples. So, naturally, they took them from the dumpster and thought of ways to sell them. Believe it or not, they went door to door selling them as mats and pot protectors. Thus, beginning their career in direct selling.

These two girls are friends to this day, 50 years later. One of them has been a top seller with AVON for over 30 years, and the other is me, Dracy. I'm here to share my journey in the direct selling industry, as a proud professional network marketer for almost 30 years.

This book has been inspired by this gorgeous girlfriend of mine's daughter, Teisha Dorianna. Teisha and I started working together almost 5 years ago when I introduced her to the company I was working with at that time. Her mother said no to holding an event for me, as it wasn't anything she thought she would like. However, her daughter Teisha was interested and said she would love to hold an event for me.

Who knew we would go full circle? Now, Teisha's mom loves the product and is a huge ambassador. That is how it all began— our coaching and mentorship became a two-way street.

Teisha is an incredible student and a fast learner. What she has done with the skills and knowledge I have taught her and what she witnessed from her mom all those years, she has been able to take it to the next level with the way the industry is growing and changing.

Teisha is the next generation. She is a top achiever and one of the top leaders in her company at the age of 25. When I was 25, I too was at the top-level breaking records, achieving awards and holidays. We are in the top 1% of Network Marketers and have a passion for making a difference and helping people say "YES" to their potential. We know this industry is a gift and we want to share our story with you, while helping you become the author of your own story by unwrapping your inner gift of leadership.

We want to share how a Gen Z / Millennial and a Gen Y / Baby Boomer navigates success in this ever-changing industry, Network Marketing. We exemplify how a Mentor and Mentee work together, learn from each other and unwrap the gifts this industry has to offer to others and the gifts inside of us.

In 2021, we decided to start supporting one another in a weekly coaching session. We work in two different companies but wanted to support one another, so we decided to make our weekly calls about a leadership focused topic and discuss what we know about it. The calls were so juicy that we decided to write a chapter each week on a topic, with no intention of a book. We wrote a list of topics we felt were important in our business. We had so much fun and excitement for our calls and accountability to write, that we discovered we were writing a book. Our insights covered a lot of ground for all ages and different levels of expertise for business builders to grow.

Along the way, we realized that this project started to unwrap our true gifts and we wanted to share them with you, while helping you become the unwrapped leader that you are.

Teisha: The Next Generation of Network Marketing & Leadership

Writing a book is something that I, Teisha, never imagined doing in a million years, even though a palm reader told me before that I would be a novelist in the future. I laughed so hard that day, but it's one memory from my past that I will always remember.

I strongly believe that everything happens for a reason. Dracy and I coming together to share our talents has been the most rewarding feeling in the world. I look up to Dracy in everything she has done to create a sustainable business that takes care of her family and friends around her.

Being able to sit down and write out my story with no intention of developing a book has helped me realize so many more gifts I have inside of me that I was born to share with you. We both only discovered what was going to come out of this writing journey about halfway through writing our story. There is nothing more raw and real about what we are sharing with you throughout this book.

Disclaimer: I'm a bit of a swear bear and I like my f-bombs. I know I can't please everybody and I've never been one to sugar coat any situation. I have a lot of passion for what I do and sometimes I express that in different ways. You can love me or hate me for it, but my intent is never to offend. The one thing I'll always be is truthful.

My initial intentions while writing was to solely help me understand my own journey and where I came from. My intentions now are to help as many new business builders as possible, see the gifted leader that they were made to be. Everyone is the author of their own story and you get to decide what happens along the way and how your story comes to an end.

For Me: Thank you for stepping outside your comfort zone and fighting through all the obstacles to get to where you are now. A dream life doesn't happen by watching from the sidelines. You are strong. You are capable. You are going to help so many people with your story. Thanks for never giving up on your dreams and for being a badass at 25 years young. I wrote a freakin' book! #FuckYeah

Whatever your reason is for picking up this book, thank you. You should be so proud to be in the Network Marketing industry. Congratulations on saying "YES" to your potential. We have no doubt that you will become an unwrapped leader in your business. We know that you'll learn more about your gifts and talents and we can't wait for you to share them with the world.

Chapter 1: The Gift of Leadership

Dracy: Become a Present Leader, Lead with Presence, Discover Your Unique Gifts and Qualities to Lead

*"Leadership is about making others better
as a result of your PRESENCE
and making sure that impact lasts in your absence."*
— *Author Unknown*

True leadership to me is when you say YES to your potential and empower others to do the same.

You are a gift waiting to be unwrapped. When you realize your presence is a gift, you will be on a journey of greatness. Nothing is more rewarding as a leader than to see your protégés grow and become leaders themselves. True leadership to me is when you say YES to your potential and empower others to do the same.

13

Let the gifts begin.

Leadership is 100% about growth. There are no shortcuts. If you have the willingness to learn, develop, and do, you will become a great leader with presence.

If you have the willingness to learn, develop, and do, you will become a great leader with presence.

Leading from within with a vision, positive attitude, and courage will give others permission to follow, lead and duplicate.

The biggest gift you can give yourself is embracing failure. By knowing that it is part of your journey, you can take it on with enthusiasm. This is what the most successful leaders have done.

Some examples include: Walt Disney, Colonel Sanders, Steven Spielberg, James Dyson, Thomas Edison, JK Rowling... the list goes on! **Why not you?**

The Network Marketing industry is the best environment to learn Leadership.

It's an environment for growth. A community of people that want for you, not from you.

14

It's a place where people want to help you become the best you can be. You can be coached, have a game plan, and a proven system, while you earn and learn.

To succeed is to learn leadership. To learn leadership, you need to develop a few key traits and skills, then repeat them, while you fix and adjust along the way.

Leadership is a gift. To become the best leader possible is to help others become and discover the leader in them. Unwrap the gifts in people and you will unwrap the leader in you.

Unwrap the gifts in people and you will unwrap the leader in you.

5 Network Marketing Gifts

1. The Gift of the Opportunity

2. The Gift of Sharing and Educating People

3. The Gift of Developing Enriched Relationships

4. The Gift of Learning Leadership Skills

5. The Gift of Becoming the Best Version of Yourself

Four Traits That You Want as a Leader

1. Be an Emotional Leader.

"You can do anything with enthusiasm.
Enthusiasm is what makes your hopes rise to the stars."
— Henry Ford

When it comes to business, act on principles— when it comes to yours and other people's dreams and achievements, act on raw and real emotions that are relevant. Be excited, enthusiastic, and proud out loud to celebrate the achievements and milestones. Sincerely praise progress and reward results.

An emotional leader will craft a vision so clear, as if it is painted like a Michelangelo painting and people will want to become a part of it and join the journey. Give your vision emotion so they can feel it, see it, and want to achieve it with YOU.

2. Be a Principle-Centered Leader.

"Trust is the glue of life. It's the most essential ingredient of effective communication. It's the foundational principle that holds relationships."
— *Steven Covey*

Leadership principles are character in action, set with guiding beliefs that are their compass. Knowing your true worth is a framework that inspires others to achieve a common goal. Be the example of learning from your failures. Do not get attached to the outcome, but fall in love with the process. Handle difficult situations, solve problems, and manage crises with kindness and correction that gives people a sense of security and trust.

A principle-centered leader does not let disappointment change their direction or decisions. They embrace change, are courageous, brave, and willing to try and learn what it takes to succeed by those before

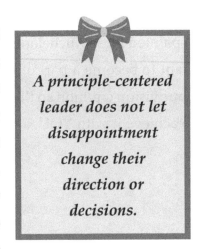

A principle-centered leader does not let disappointment change their direction or decisions.

them. They learn the art of responding vs reacting to

18

all situations and are prepared to be bad before they are good and good before they are great. Humility is their friend. Their mindset is their diamond mine that needs to be fiercely protected for productivity.

3. Be a Present Leader

"At the end of the day, people won't remember what you said or did, they will remember how you made them feel."
— *Maya Angelou*

A present leader has a philosophy of being of service and doing what it takes to make people feel special, heard, and valued. They will always use your name, look you in the eye and be interested and honest with you. They will be present in your conversation, with no distraction.

A present leader will seek to know your family situation, hobbies, passions, and goals. They will show you the way vs tell you the way and do whatever it takes not to let you down. They will follow up and follow through on any commitments and conversations you may have had. Integrity and trust are some of their highest values.

4. Be a Disciplined Leader

"There are 2 kinds of pain.
The pain of discipline and the pain of regret.
Discipline weighs pennies, regret weighs tons."
— Jim Rohn

Discipline comes from good old fashioned healthy habits, mind-body, and spirit. A disciplined leader focuses on their income-producing habits, their daily disciplines in all areas of their life, and sets goals with accountability. They lead from within by crafting and creating their triumph story and most importantly, overcoming the hurdles and hardship along the way.

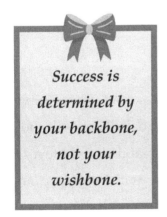

Success is determined by your backbone, not your wishbone.

Success is determined by your backbone, not your wishbone. Disciplined leaders fuel their leadership with experience, action, and execution. They will rehearse, review and repeat daily, weekly and quarterly. Everything is measured by activities and results.

What you lack in skills can be made up for in numbers.

20

Seek to get help and answers.

Skills Required to Build a Network Marketing Empire

- Art of Storytelling
- Presentations
- Call to Actions
- Closing
- Creating the Sense of Urgency
- Selling your Position
- Engaging, Educating, Enrolling, Empowering
- Appreciating People, the way they feel valued
- Onboarding New Distributors
- Creating Leaders
- Personal Branding Online & Offline
- Social Media

Make the Decision

You can become a present leader by just making the decision. Once you make that decision, you become a leader in training for a lifetime. Attach yourself to a mentor/coach and take the steps to the biggest gift you can give someone: the gift of Leadership.

"A sign of a true leader is not by how many followers they have, but how many leaders they have created."
— *Mahatma Gandhi*

I started in the Network Marketing Industry 27 years ago. I became a leader in 90 days following the system. I earned $5,000 in my first month as a leader, in 12 months promoted out 12 leaders, earned over $100,000, and 5 years later, earned over 1 million dollars while developing a multi-million-dollar business with hundreds of leaders and a 23-year career with one company.

That was coming from being a single mom on welfare with a drive to become independent. I remember standing in the bank line up to cash a welfare cheque. I remember that feeling, and at that moment I knew I never wanted to rely on the system again.

That night I saw a Tony Robbins infomercial about Awaken The Giant Within: that was my ticket. I couldn't afford to buy his cassette series, so I went to the library and checked out one cassette at a time, out of 12. I listened to them one at a time.

It was enough to commit to making personal development and leadership as my life project. I found something I was passionate about. I did not have to put my daughter in daycare. I wasn't with a company at that time, but I was open and ready for an opportunity. Up leveling was the best gift I gave myself.

30 years later, I continue to earn a full-time 6 figure income, I live an above average life, I raised 4 children as the sole income earner, I've traveled the world, and I am able to be present in all the things that matter.

Let me introduce to you just one of my most prized protégés. She is an Unwrapped Leader, and what a *gift* she has been to my life and so many around her. This is her story and our lessons in how you can develop the skills, work on yourself and develop your gifts to unwrap the leader in you. Whether it is in Network Marketing, running your own business, becoming an influencer or just becoming a better person, all these skills will make a difference in *you*.

Teisha: Accidental Leadership

If you would've asked me how I felt about leadership four years ago, I would've told you that I wasn't capable. I would've told you that I was far too shy and quiet to lead a group of people. I was your typical "follower." I was the one in group projects who needed to be told what to do. I enjoyed working behind the scenes and letting others take the lead on presentations and group projects.

I literally wanted to do *anything else* than have to present in front of a crowd or give my opinion and thoughts in front of a group of people. What if they didn't like what I had to say? What if they laughed at me? What if I was wrong? Those were the fearful thoughts that ran through my head throughout Junior High, High School, and most of my time in university.

For all of my school projects that required a presentation, I asked my teacher how much that portion was worth. Whatever it was, I told them to take that percentage off my final grade because I would not present in front of the class. Most of my teachers made exceptions for me to present just in front of them during my lunch hour. I took it.

What to Do After Graduation?

I wanted *nothing* to do with being in front of a group of people. I never lifted my hand up in class to answer anything. If I'm being perfectly honest, I didn't like school. I worked extremely hard for the most mediocre grades.

I had no idea what the heck I was going to do after graduating. In fact, I was in a career cruising program to discover what to do after graduation. I checked off my likes and dislikes throughout the quiz. I remember answering "dislike" to almost everything school related. It just wasn't interesting to me.

After taking the quiz, the website displayed my top ten career options. I can't remember much of what options were given to me, but one career stuck out like a sore thumb at that moment. A f*cking circus clown! Are you kidding me!? I was set out to be a circus clown?!

I re-did that test. I pretended to like math and some other subjects that I didn't actually enjoy, just to get a better list. Bam! My top ten options changed. The careers "teacher" and "nurse" pop up. I knew I couldn't be a nurse. I'm terrified of blood and needles. That's out. A teacher? I didn't have experience with kids, but

I could teach elementary school! I would feel like the smartest person in the room. I had patience. I chose to do my research paper on an elementary school teacher. It seemed like a valid option at the time.

I transitioned into high school and was still the same shy person from junior high. You might be a friend of mine reading this and thinking, "Teisha is not shy." I was very outgoing when it came to my friends and anything related to sports. The shyness presented itself within the classroom more than anything.

This was the age where my parents suggested I find a summer job to keep me busy and make some extra income for the future. I decided to apply at a daycare. This provided me with extra income and gave me more experience with kids. I volunteered coaching youth soccer in the summers throughout high school. I enjoyed my daycare job, and coaching. I worked in two different daycares during high school, and coached youth soccer in the summer for five years.

After graduating high school, I decided to go to university for elementary teaching. I was unsure and continuously thought, "I just went to school for my entire life so far, just to go back to school for the rest of my life." Umm, read that over again.

I wanted to get out of my small town and move to the city. I was in university for five years. I graduated with a Bachelor of Arts degree, majoring in Psychology and a Bachelor of Elementary Education degree by the time I was 22 years old. You may think that's a huge accomplishment. The amount I learned and grew as a person in those five years was huge. I stepped outside my comfort zone every day to become more confident.

When I decided to go for elementary teaching, I did not realize I would be giving multiple presentations in front of people that were much older than me. I was one of the youngest in my graduating class.

The way we were taught is that if you want to learn how to do something, jump in and do it. University was a huge deal. I couldn't refuse to present because they would fail me. I learned how to present in my final years. This was the most difficult thing I had done in my life up to that point. I never enjoyed my classes that much, but I have zero regrets about going to university for teaching. However, I still never felt fulfilled after graduating. It didn't feel right that I was going to do this for the rest of my life. Just imagine what my parents thought after I told them that.

A Surprising Opportunity & Skill

Let's rewind a couple years. I was introduced to a Network Marketing company in my final two years of university by my mom's friend, Dracy. It was a loose leaf tea and wellness company. I had never been a coffee drinker, but I always loved my tea. This was right up my alley. I decided to host my own event at my place in the city with my friends and family members. It was a blast. I was excited to try real iced fruit tea for the first time. I didn't even know it was a thing. You can make loose leaf teas iced and they tasted delicious?! Who knew!

I received a ton of free and discounted products from my event, because my sales did so well. That's when Dracy decided to share this business opportunity with me. Was I looking for a job? Definitely not — I was a full-time university student in my final practicum. I did not have time for this, but I was still open to listening. After hearing about how flexible it was, and to think I could do most of it from my phone and laptop in between classes, I thought, "Why not?" If I got some free tea out of this, I would be happy. That was my only goal when I started.

28

My network marketing business became part of my life. Dracy asked me if I would be interested in building my own team like her. My answer was no. Me leading a team? I don't think so.

In my first year, I continued to use the product and share my love for tea with others. I ran online events for others right from my phone— online events were my favorite. Then, something strange happened. People approached me, inquiring about the business. This was exciting. To think, someone wanted to do this with me.

My first prospect signed up. Then another person, and another, and another. I reached the first Leadership rank in my company. At the time, I thought, "This has to be a mistake. I didn't do anything. I never asked these people to join me. I'm an accidental leader now."

Then, boom! I approached a near full-time business income. I was no longer getting tea at a discount. I paid off my entire semester of school. How was this happening to me? Once again, I thought, "I'm not doing anything! I'm just having fun!"

My team size continued to grow. I kept up with their questions and ensured their success starting out, just like me. Was I really becoming a leader?

My network marketing business was on the priority list. I loved the extra income, the small community I was building, and I loved the products. I came home from my dreaded practicum and worked on my business every day. At this point, it was the only thing keeping me sane.

I struggled mentally during my final practicum. I was placed in an unsupportive environment and came home crying almost daily. I never thought about quitting teaching because I was determined to complete my practicum and receive my degree. I was mentally struggling so much that I would make myself physically sick and I wouldn't be able to get up in the mornings to go. I missed a whole week and had to make up for that time at the end of my practicum.

The only thing I enjoyed any more was my business. My family and friends said I should take a break from my tea business to focus on my practicum. All I thought was, "I invested a lot of time and energy into a business I loved to get to where I am right now, and I don't intend on stopping now. Why would I risk losing everything I've built when it's the only thing I enjoy?"

Although I was putting a lot of time and focus into my business, I loved every second of it. It began as a hobby and grew into a full-time job with a part-time income in such little time. Getting paid for doing something I loved blew me away. I never stopped working on my business. I finished my final practicum and graduated with an excellent grade when I was at my lowest mental state.

I never attended graduation, and never pursued full-time teaching. It just didn't feel right. I chose to pursue my network marketing business full time and substitute-teach on the side strictly for extra income.

That year was a gamble. What if I didn't make it work? Was I capable of being a true leader to my team? Would it only last a few months until my old, shy self chose to take over?

I didn't know what would happen, but I knew I had never been so passionate about anything in my life. Network Marketing brought me the most happiness I've ever experienced. I could have had a full-time teaching position, making double what I was making with my business at the time.

I applied for teaching positions right after graduating because it was the natural next step. However, when I got the calls to go for some interviews, I turned them all down. I knew I could have had a job. I knew other teachers out there would have loved to have a full-time position that year.

It just didn't feel right, and here's why: you know when people say happiness is so much more important than money will ever be? Most people will agree with that statement but I don't think people truly understand what it means until they're put in a situation where they absolutely hate what they're doing and how they feel.

I was desperate to make this work. I never wanted to go back to my teaching career after what I had experienced. I pushed myself to show up consistently, learn more, and be the best damn leader out there I could ever be. It paid off.

Network Marketing gave me leadership skills, courage, confidence, financial freedom, a sense of belonging, and most importantly, happiness. I was surprised to find myself earning a VIP trip for two to Punta Cana just after my first year.

It was unbelievable. I thought, "How is this happening to someone like me? Someone who started from zero. Someone who lacked so much confidence in herself. Someone who used to think she wasn't capable of being a leader." It was time for my first conference. I was receiving excellence awards.

I was the number one recruiter in the entire company. I also ranked number two in the entire company for personal sales. At that moment, I thought, "WTF!? Is this a joke? Am I doing anything special? I don't think so!" I was asked to lead a training session on recruiting for the entire company. I was about to throw up, but I said yes, because how could I pass that up? I attended my first conference and led my training. I still haven't overcome my fear of public speaking. I have simply learned to publicly speak in fear.

I'm excited to dive deeper into my story throughout this book, but here's the lesson: Leadership is created, not found. I was not born with the skills I have today.

All this time, I thought I was doing nothing.

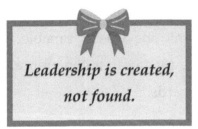

Leadership is created, not found.

I thought I was an "accidental leader" because I wasn't asking people to join me. All I knew going into my business was I loved a product and wanted others to love it as much as me. I showed up authentically and unapologetically myself every day. I naturally attracted people to me because of how passionate I was about what I was doing.

I was meant to be a leader all along. I only needed to step outside my comfort zone to realize I had it in me. Anyone is capable of leadership if they have the courage to step outside their comfort

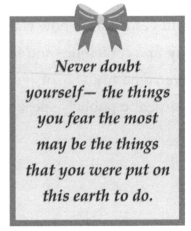

Never doubt yourself— the things you fear the most may be the things that you were put on this earth to do.

zone and want it. Leadership is the gift that changed my life forever. It has helped me unwrap my passion

34

and the confidence within me. Never doubt yourself—
the things you fear the most may be the things you
were put on this earth to do. Everyone has the gift of
leadership within them. It's your time to unwrap the
gift within yourself. Your journey begins with a
purpose.

Chapter 2: The Gift of a Strong Mindset

Teisha: Who, What, When, Where, Why

- **Who?** A strong mindset appears in people who believe what they have to offer is incredible.
- **What?** A strong mindset is a strong belief system that keeps you from quitting when things get tough.
- **When?** A strong mindset develops when you can prioritize your own thoughts & feelings, rather than focusing on others'.
- **Where?** A strong mindset is required in order to sell your products, programs & position to people online and offline.
- **Why?** A strong mindset is important because without one, you lack a healthy self-esteem & confidence in yourself.

Your Mindset is Your Biggest Asset

I lacked confidence in myself growing up. I wasn't confident because I never had a strong belief system. I was a follower and went with the flow. My mindset was weak. I was easily swayed and was content being told what to do and think.

I lacked the motivation to learn about several topics throughout my school days. It bothered me, though. You tend to grow a strong mindset for what you're deeply passionate about. For example, I loved sports. I played all of them and knew I had talent in those areas. I was named athlete of the year in Junior High. No one could tell me what to think or do when playing sports. I did what felt right and I played the game with passion.

I had patience in team sports but found it hard to control my emotions in individual sports. For instance, I was always the teammate cheering on others in sports like Volleyball and Basketball. But when it came to Singles Badminton, I would easily "get down on myself" when I was losing a game. I would let it get so far into my head by thinking I wasn't good enough.

Soon enough, it reflected in my actions. I would give up. Why even try? I cried after losing a match. It was embarrassing. I had such a weak mindset in sports.

When I moved on to university, I attended badminton tryouts. I made the team and learned so much in the three years I played. I was playing next-level players who completely crushed me. It was insane. But one important thing my coach taught me was to always keep my head in the game and remember why I'm doing what I'm doing. I came to tryouts for a reason. I made the team for a reason. I loved sports for a reason. I needed to remember my purpose in those moments. Changing my mentality and remembering why I'm doing this made the biggest difference in my skills. This is when I began to grow.

It's the same when it comes to Network Marketing. Your mindset is the biggest asset in your business. The difference between the people who

Your mindset is the biggest asset in your business.

succeed and those who fail lies within their mindset.

You Can Never Fail

Here's the thing: you can never "fail" at Network Marketing unless you physically try to. Growing a successful business takes time. If your mindset isn't strong enough, in the beginning, to get you through the obstacles you'll face, then you will create a negative story about the circumstance you are in.

For example, let's say you speak to 9 people about your business opportunity, and they say no. Someone without a strong mindset would say, "This is impossible and way too much work. I'm giving up because I'm not good at this." It is the negative story they chose to create about themselves. That's how you fail at Network Marketing. The circumstance was neutral. The weak mindset chose to create a negative story from it.

Someone who speaks to the same nine people with a strong mindset would say, "I am getting so close to getting my first yes. I'm not quitting now." The strong mindset turned the same neutral circumstance into a positive story. As a result, the strong mindset performed positive actions and recruited their first team member. Statistically, 1 in every 10 people you share the business opportunity with will sign up with you. The person with the weak mindset gave up moments before the magic was about to happen. Be patient. It feels hard because you're new at it, not because you suck.

You must believe that what you have to offer is freaking incredible, or you will not grow.

One of the best pieces of advice I give my team: you must believe what you have to offer is freaking incredible, or you will not grow.

If you were unsure your product could help someone, why would they purchase from you? If you didn't believe your customer rewards program was an incredible freaking deal, why would anyone else believe that? If you don't believe your business opportunity can change lives, why would anyone join you? The answer is they will not buy your product, host, or join your team because your mindset and belief system are not strong enough.

If you're reading this thinking, "I honestly can't get behind my product and services," then it's time to get out, friend. Passion goes a long way, and that's a red flag you do not have it with what you're doing right now.

Ask Yourself...

If you want to be a successful Network Marketer, shift your mindset when having conversations with people. Let's start with sales. Ask yourself, "Are you offering them an incredible product and could potentially solve a problem of theirs? Or, do you want them to buy it because it helps you?"

You better believe your product will improve their life in one way or another. Otherwise, wave goodbye to a good sales month. Ask yourself, "Do you believe offering them the opportunity to book an event with you will improve their life in some way? Or are you just hoping to hit your goal for the month?" Maybe it's a favor someone is doing for you to help you reach your goal. It's disappointing you don't believe your programs will serve them.

Ask yourself, "Do I think my business opportunity could change their life or improve their current lifestyle? Or are you just desperate to have your first teammate join you regardless of their intentions with the business? A kitnapper, of course I'll take them! A number is a number. A "kitnapper" is someone who joins a Network Marketing business with the intent of getting a kit with discounted products and doing nothing else.

What's the Point?

If you found yourself comparing your answers to the one that mostly involved what's in it for you, you're doing it wrong. Start coming from the point of service in everything you do. Instead of looking at it as they're doing you a favor, shift your mindset. You're doing them a favor by offering an incredible product or program. The mindset shift makes a *huge* difference in your business. I promise you!

Without a strong mindset, you don't have anything. The biggest turning point in my business was when someone told me to focus only on what I had control over. Try not to get worked up about what you cannot do anything about. When I started focusing on the factors I could control, my business changed.

I no longer get angry when a product doesn't arrive in good condition. This happens in every business! What's the point in getting mad? I no longer got angry when a teammate decided to randomly quit even though I thought they were going to be my next "rockstar." I can't control people's feelings. Wasn't I doing this leadership thing to make a difference? Wasn't I doing this to make an impact and help improve the lifestyles of others? If someone lacks motivation or passion for what they do, shouldn't I encourage them to find what they're passionate about? The best people in this world are those with a strong passion. If someone is miserable at their job, I feel sorry for them. I wouldn't wish that on anyone. I truly want the best for people. My job is to help you discover the things you are capable of.

Dracy: Mindset is The Movie You Choose to Play in Your Head

You have a choice between two stories. The story you tell yourself, or "The Perfect Story."

The next time someone asks you how you are doing, what you are up to, or what you are working on, pay attention to the story you tell them. If someone offers you an exciting opportunity or the opportunity to try something new, what is your response? If you have wanted something for a very long time and someone asked you why you don't have it yet, what is the story you tell them?

Here is a story that reminds me we have a choice.

"A Cherokee Legend of Two Wolves"

An old Cherokee is teaching his grandson about life. "A fight is going on inside me," he said to the boy. "It is a terrible fight and it is between two wolves. One is evil— anger, envy, sorrow, regret, greed, arrogance, self-pity, guilt, resentment, inferiority, lies, false pride, superiority, and ego." He continued, "The other is good— joy, peace, love, hope, serenity, humility,

45

kindness, benevolence, empathy, generosity, truth, compassion, and faith. The same fight continues inside you— and inside every other person."

The grandson thought about it for a minute and then asked his grandfather, "Which wolf will win?"

The old Cherokee simply replied, "The one you feed."

Two Types of Mindsets

Love Mindset: Love is open, focuses on growth. Willingness to try new things.

Fear Mindset: Fear is fixed, afraid and not willing to try anything. Makes excuses.

Nature & Nurture

Here's a new way of approaching every opportunity.

Two brothers were told to go to the barn, ask no questions, just wait until Dad was to arrive and give them instructions of what to do. In the barn, they discovered a wheelbarrow full of manure. While they sat there silently waiting for their father, one brother could only think about how much manure there was and how much work there was going to be. The longer he sat, the more anxious he got about the workload and expectations. The other brother was smiling, excited and could not contain himself. All he could think was, if this is horse manure, Dad must have bought a horse.

Nature is your inherent qualities, who you are at the core. Your nature is naturally positive or negative. Optimistic or pessimistic. Think about possibilities versus what can go wrong.

Ask yourself what your nature is when it comes to taking on anything new.

Nurture is to support and encourage. A period of educating, training, or development— and it can be learned.

47

What is exciting is no matter what your nature is, it can be nurtured. *If you choose.* Accepting your nature is the first step to a growth mindset.

Accepting your nature is the first step to a growth mindset.

You can nurture your thoughts with tender care.

The National Science Foundation states an average person has 12,000 to 60,000 thoughts per day. 80% of those are negative and 95% are repetitive thoughts. If we repeat those negative thoughts, we think negative way more than we think positive thoughts.

Nurturing your thoughts takes training.

Nurturing your thoughts takes training. Like a sport, training requires three (must haves) keys to success: good instruction, practice, and repetition.

8 Steps to Training Your Brain Into A Diamond Mind

1. Create a clear picture of the desired outcome

2. Remove the mental mists / myths that linger in your head

3. Develop a growth mindset with meditation and a mentor

4. Replace negative people, places, or perceptions with positive ones

5. Daily affirmations of the person you need to become to achieve the desired result

6. Practice, Drill & Rehearse the actions mentally and physically

7. Be prepared for the obstacles and objections to overcome

8. Resilience: bouncing back from adversity, disappointment, and failure instead of giving up

What is Your Perfect Story?

To write a great script or be a director of an all-time blockbuster, you need specific elements to make the "Perfect Story."

The best and most empowering stories are those that overcame adversity, hardship, or personal warfare. Conflict, growth, and transformation are all worthy stories. How did you turn your ordinary life into an extraordinary one? This is what people want to hear about and learn how you overcame these challenges. We always look for strong characters who make a difference and touch hearts.

The best and most empowering stories are those that overcame adversity, hardship, or personal warfare.

The start of your perfect story starts with the main character. What characteristics and mindset will yours have?

Will yours have a Diamond Mind?

"Shine bright like a Diamond." — Rihanna

6 Traits and Characteristics associated with a positive mindset that allow your Diamond Mind to SHINE

Optimism: a willingness to make an effort and take a chance instead of assuming your efforts won't pay off.

Acceptance: acknowledging things don't always turn out how you want them to, but learning from your mistakes.

Resilience: bouncing back from adversity, disappointment, and failure instead of giving up.

Gratitude: actively, continuously appreciating the good things in your life.

Consciousness/Mindfulness: dedicating the mind to conscious awareness and enhancing the ability to focus.

Integrity: the trait of being honorable, righteous, and straightforward, instead of deceitful and self-serving (Power of Positivity, n.d.).

Chapter 3: The Gift of Confidence

Teisha: Radiate Positivity & Passion

"Confidence comes not from always being right, but from not fearing to be wrong."
— Peter T. McIntyre

Remember when you were a kid and were unapologetically *yourself*? You just did whatever you wanted to do and didn't care what others thought. People smiled when they saw you. People laughed at your goofiness. People loved you for exactly who you were. Then, you grew up and people pointed out their own insecurities. You learned what was accepted and frowned upon. You discovered "beauty standards" through magazines, social media, and tv.

All of a sudden, you wanted to change: Change in appearance. Change in personality. Change made you more likable, just like the person you saw on Instagram. You associated popularity with certain people, appearances, and physical items such as brand names. You believed once you acquired the "perfect" appearance, personality, and physical items, you would finally be happy and confident in yourself— but in the long run, that's not true!

Once you get into the comparison game, you never win. You compare yourself to others and it feels like you are never enough.

Once you get into the comparison game, you never win.

The True Key to Confidence

If you're feeling insecure right now about who you are and what you look like, how can you change that feeling without changing yourself? How can you truly be the best version of yourself?

When you stop caring about what other people think of you and start focusing on what brings you happiness, magical things happen. You are now doing things for you, not for anybody else. Have you ever heard the saying you cannot pour from an empty cup?

It's 100% true. If you can't learn to accept yourself, how could you expect others to?

My favorite kinds of people always radiated positivity and passion— always smiling. They see the good in every situation. I always wanted to be like that. They had confidence. Is confidence just natural to some people? Are people just born with it? Can it be learned? I'm going to share my story with you on how I went from a shy, insecure girl to a happy, passionate, and confident woman.

Growing up, I was shy. Not so shy around my friends, but shy when it came to speaking up in school and giving my opinion. I preferred to not have an opinion at all. The less came out of my mouth, the less chance someone could judge me. I was quiet in class and preferred someone else take the lead in group projects as I mentioned earlier. I was okay with people telling me what I could do to help and how I should do it.

As a result of this, I never performed well with presentations, especially when solo. I had to create my own opinion and thoughts on a topic, and share them with the class. Uhhh, no thanks! The fear of being wrong or saying something inaccurate was soooo real.

Fast Forward to University

I chose to pursue an elementary teaching career. But why? It's simple:

1. I babysat growing up, worked in a couple daycares, and enjoyed being around children.

2. I couldn't teach Junior High or High School because I was a mediocre student myself growing up. No one could be smarter than me, especially in my career. If I taught elementary, I could ensure I would always know more than them.

Those were my thoughts. I thought I couldn't open up my mouth unless I was correct. I thought being a teacher meant I wasn't allowed to be wrong or make mistakes.

This is how insecure I was about myself. I felt scared I would never be enough. Little did I know I would be presenting to other adults even older than me in university.

Time to face my fears! This time, I simply had to do it. I thought, "If I wanted a decent career, I need a degree!" There was no time to ensure everything was perfect. I needed to learn by doing, which meant making mistakes.

I faced millions of fear barriers throughout university. Throughout my practicums, I learned the lesson the day before, then taught it the next day. Was I an expert? Absolutely not. Did I make mistakes? *Many!*

For instance, a grade 5 student asked me if it was winter all around the world at that time. Not even thinking, I assumed "yes" and rolled with it, to later discover I was giving false information. AHHH! How embarrassing! A student argued with me it was not winter in all countries, but I still stuck with it. Yikes, an elementary student outsmarting me?! This was my BIGGEST fear!

My Biggest Fears

There was another instance where a student asked me where a country was on the map. I had no clue— I'm brutal at geography. I decided to respond, "I'm not too sure." Reply: "You're the teacher. Aren't you supposed to know?" I laugh now, but in the moment, it was a huge fear of mine. I felt stupid and insecure. I thought elementary school would be the *easy* route, but boy was I wrong! I faced many challenges.

Although I faced many of my fears throughout university, I didn't overcome them. I simply learned to do these things in fear. It wasn't until I was introduced to the Network Marketing industry I found my confidence and discovered who I was meant to help.

My mentor and co-author, Dracy Dewar, was the lovely woman who introduced me to this industry. Although my mom had been in the industry for 25 years at the time, I was not asked to consider it myself until Dracy came along.

I wondered how I would pull this off. Me, a salesperson? That's what I was going to be, right? I couldn't even speak in public. How would I sell something to someone?

I Began Knowing Only Two Things...

I was wrong about many assumptions in Network Marketing. This industry is simply a personal growth program with a compensation plan attached. I began my business only knowing two things: I loved the product and so did my family and friends.

I started by doing most of my business online. I did online events, ran my social media accounts, & created an online community.

When originally asked by Dracy how I felt about leadership and building my team, the answer was simple: I have no desire to lead a team, nor could I see myself being a leader. It was not my style. It sounded "pushy." I continued to only do what I loved, within my comfort zone. I lacked confidence in myself.

However, when I spoke about the products with others and shared my passion, I noticed a more confident version of myself. I loved the feeling of leading an event and getting to know people.

After almost a year in the business, I began to naturally attract people to what I was doing. I later discovered that I was in fact not an accidental leader. This is what leadership should look like. It should come from having fun and being your genuine self. It should not be pushy or annoying. If it is, you're doing it wrong.

It's about that belief in what you do. Believe that what you have to offer is absolutely amazing. Be selfless. Offer others the same opportunity you were offered. You never know what someone else needs in that moment of their life.

If you think Network Marketing is just a way to make extra income, you are so wrong. This industry completely changed my life. I finally feel like I'm exactly where I belong. I am happy. I have financial comfort. I feel confident. I feel proud to impact others. I feel like a true leader. I'm living proof you can make it to the top and be your best self, even when you feel like you're starting at zero with no experience.

It just takes a little bit of courage to get started and an open mind combined with a positive attitude. If you can uncover those qualities, you can gain confidence in yourself.

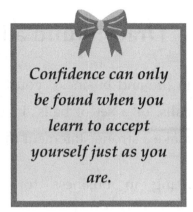

Confidence can only be found when you learn to accept yourself just as you are.

Confidence can only be found when you learn to accept yourself just as you are.

Dracy: Build a Ballsy Business

In life and business, you must be bold and have big balls, or a set of balls. I say this in complete fun, to make a strong statement that you will not forget.

Being in business for almost 30 years as an independent woman, coach, leader and rockstar, I have been the sole income earner. I have raised three strong daughters, and one son— confident kids with natural leadership qualities. I taught them not to take things personally or literally, but to listen to the intent. I share this because this term has been used for courage and bravery.

Two of the most admired qualities of all time. Courage and bravery. "Character" wins over many faults and failures. Be confident in yourself— believe you are bold and brave— or at least be in the pursuit of it.

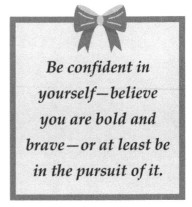

Be confident in yourself—believe you are bold and brave—or at least be in the pursuit of it.

I teach this to myself, my kids, and everyone I have worked with.

Consider Lucille Ball and her character. Lucille Ball is gifted with natural leadership and the capacity to accumulate great wealth. She has a great talent for management in all walks of life, especially in business and financial matters, where she contributes the greater vision, purpose, and long-range goals.

You don't all have to be Lucy, but what are the characteristics and skills she embodied that made her the success she is? Lucille had to be careful of becoming stubborn, intolerant, overbearing, and impatient. I admire how she was able to manage her strengths and weaknesses through all of her opportunities and threats.

Become the Person You Want to Be

Who do you admire? What characteristics do you admire about them?

Are these characteristics that you embody or would like to embody? The best part is, you can. These are the skills you can use to become the person you want to be. You can acquire the focus, motivation, dedication and success you seek from the experts who have already trail blazed before you, and finally arrive at the best chapter of your life.

In an earlier chapter of my own, years ago, I had a long overwhelming list of attributes that I wanted to improve. I tackled one quality every three months. I created an affirmation around that quality; every day I practiced, drilled and rehearsed it until it became one of my gifts.

How do you have the best chapter of your life with so much noise around you?

No matter how intimidating or hard any project seems, personally or professionally, **show up.** That's the hardest part. After you show up, your nature (and the momentum of others) forces you to **step up.** In time, your confidence grows, and you naturally stand out.

You don't have to be the best, the fastest, or even very good— just have a character that stands out, and the divine laws of nature will take its course for your success.

In business and life, you must develop skills— which you can learn with the right attitude, mindset, and support.

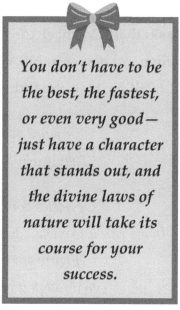

You don't have to be the best, the fastest, or even very good— just have a character that stands out, and the divine laws of nature will take its course for your success.

Become a Great Professional Athlete

Consider your favorite athlete. What makes that person a success, including their makeup, character, and performance? How does that athlete leave a mark on your mind and soul?

Basketball: Michael Jordan. Jordan became the first billionaire player in NBA history. With a net worth of $1.6 billion, he is the fifth-richest African American.

"I've failed over and over again.
That is why I succeed in life."

"Obstacles don't have to stop you.
If you run into a wall, don't turn around and give up.
Figure out how to climb it,
go through it or work around it."

"You can practice shooting eight hours a day,
but if your technique is wrong
then all you become is shooting the wrong way.
Get the fundamentals down
and the level of everything you do will rise."

Basketball makes you run, jump, change directions. Teamwork and the individual matter equally. Every minute counts and the game never stops. You can learn the fundamentals in a few days.

Practice, Practice, Practice. Rules are not complicated-everyone can learn to play basketball. That is why I have always worked in a team environment, taking everyone's talents together to achieve more. If I didn't have a team, I created one.

Baseball: Babe Ruth dominated the game, amassing numbers that had never been seen before. He changed baseball from a grind-it-out style to one of power and high-scoring games. He rewrote the record books from a "hitting" standpoint, combining a high batting average with unbelievable power. The result was an assault on baseball's most hallowed records. Despite passing over 60 years ago, Babe still remains the greatest figure in major league baseball.

"You can't beat the person who never gives up."

"Yesterday's home runs don't win today's games."

"Don't let the fear of striking out hold you back."

Baseball's uniqueness to life is to expect curveballs. Be prepared for them. Baseball is a game in which even the very best hitters fail more than 50% of the time. A home run is the most exciting moment in any sport. Baseball isn't a rush to the finish. Baseball is relaxed and carefree- it decides when it wants to end.

Like you, I have had a lot of curve balls in my life, personally and professionally. By applying these principles of preparation, you and I can be less affected. When I hit a home run, everyone feels it, not just me.

You are in control of your game when you have support and preparation.

Golf: Tiger Woods, at age nine, made a bold commitment to his father. "I'm going to be professionally excellent."

Since turning professional in 1996, Tiger built an unprecedented competitive career. His achievements on the course— 106 worldwide wins and 15 majors— have mirrored his success off the course as well.

"The bigger the setback, the greater the comeback."

*"The great thing about tomorrow is,
I will be better than I am today."*

"My main focus is on my game."

Golf: is a sport that requires concentration and precision, a reminder for you to keep your "eye on the ball" and remain focused. This sport requires great drive, balance and connecting the ball. Take these qualities seriously, especially achieving goals you set for yourself, and helping others achieve theirs.

The drive is what gives us the distance getting on that green, but the focus is what gets us in the hole. Many times, when you set a goal, it seems so far away, but you must stay the course. It doesn't matter how many times you must hit that ball. Focus and learn from every hit, in order to improve.

When on the green, the goal is to get the ball in the hole, with as few shots as possible. You need the most focus. This final stage can take more "shots" than it took you to get on that green, if you are not careful. This can be very frustrating. Focus on that hole, balance all your energy into the stance, the connection and swing, and you will not only get that par, birdie, or eagle, or even a hole-in-one. Stay the course. Keep playing!

Tennis: Serena Williams revolutionized women's tennis with her powerful style of play and won more Grand Slam singles titles than any other woman or man during the open era.

She is the strongest woman to ever play the game.

"I really think a champion is defined not by their wins but how they can recover when they fall."

"Whatever I fear inside me, my desire to win is always stronger."

"Don't be afraid to give up the good to go for the great."

Tennis is a lifetime sport. Like business, you need stamina, back and forth, constant movement, and action. Highly competitive, a game of tennis involves a variety of types of play, including serving the ball, fast movements, and strategic gameplay. Much like cricket or chess, tennis is one of the longest running games, but requires a strong mental skill.

Even with excessive mental preparation, you still never know what your opponent may do. You must be incredibly resilient and responsive. Know how you are going to play out each situation. You will learn a lot about people. Everyone's nature is to react to anything— the good, the bad and the ugly.

If you can learn and teach others how to respond to any situation by using their "head" and the goal of a positive outcome, you win games, and get Grand Slams.

Volleyball: Charles "Karc" Kiraly is the Michael Jordan, Wayne Gretzky, Babe Ruth of volleyball. Kiraly dominated indoor volleyball to the tune of three Olympic gold medals, and claimed the beach volleyball gold medal. He's the only person to win gold in both versions of the sport. Kiraly is the best volleyball player of the century.

"No volleyball play can begin without the serve and the serve is the only technique that is totally under your control. In other endeavors, you cannot succeed without believing in yourself. That belief is completely in your control."

"Practice like it's a competition and compete like it's another day on the practice court."

"We are all going to fall short, we are all going to have some bitter losses, very painful defeats and failures. We

have to use those to come back even stronger. That's what makes it sweeter. Then we can overcome those and figure out a way to win. Great teams can do that. As those are gold medal winning teams."

Volleyball requires a quick reaction time and good anticipation skills. It's about quick changes in direction. The core is the foundation of everything players do. The serve sets up the game. Each player has a specific job to do. Each position works with other teammates to make the best play possible.

In business, your goal and role is to serve. Greatness will follow. It is the natural law. Each day I ask myself, "How can I be of service to the world?" In any challenging situation, ask yourself, "How can I serve?" Make your serve great and you will become one of the greats.

Soccer: Diego Maradona was extremely skilled. His dribbling ability was mesmerizing, his goal-scoring was clinical, passing and crossing were precise — earning him many assists in his career. From attacking midfield, he scored 345 goals in 680 games.

"My mother thinks that I am the best. I was raised to believe what my mother tells me."

"When people succeed it is because of hard work. Luck has nothing to do with success."

"All the people that criticized me can eat their words."

Soccer teaches coordination and on-the-run thinking. It promotes teamwork and sharing. Soccer is about the collective effort towards a single goal, requiring technique, mindset and game intelligence.

What is your single goal? Who do you need to achieve this goal? You cannot win championships alone. What skills do you need to work on? How will you become the great professional business athlete you were born to be?

Three Steps to Grabbing Life By the Balls

1. Predict your Future. VISION. What if you are in control of your future? You don't need any fortune teller to tell you your future. Have a vision for your future! Predict, plan, prepare. Live the life you imagine. Visualize what you love to do, with the people you love to do them with, where you want to do them.

Life is far too precious to just let things happen. Instead, make things happen. You are the star in your story. Write that story before others write it about

Life is far too precious to just let things happen. Instead, make things happen.

you. Those with vision are great leaders. Others follow brave visionaries.

2. Plan and Prepare. The biggest driver to my success is *support*. I attribute my accomplishments to having a great coach who was tough, committed, and believed in me. The only times I was stagnant in my life or business were the times I did not have a coach.

74

A coach must be committed to you, the support of good leadership, and teamwork. You need cheerleaders and a fan club, but this will come on its own natural merits- let them find and follow you.

3. Take Action. Join the circus. Go from juggling those balls to becoming the world's greatest showman.

Life will challenge you to lose your marbles and ball your eyes out a time or two, but if you stay away from the goofballs, you will succeed, celebrate your achievement, and maybe even attend a ball.

Character and performance over time is the essence of becoming a *great professional business athlete.*

Have a ball. Do you want to leave a mark in the minds and souls of those around you? Are you tired of playing B-rated ball? Are you ready for the big leagues? Is now your time? You need a coach that can take you to the playoffs and win— who will assess your strengths and weaknesses, work through your opportunities that lay ahead, and help create a great game plan that works through the threats, so you become 10 feet tall and bulletproof.

Chapter 4: The Gift of Patience

Teisha: Teachers Must Have Hated Me...

Patience is arguably the most important quality you can have as a Network Marketer. This will help you succeed through every single stage in this industry. Before I get into how you can have patience to be successful, I want to share my story around patience and how it helped me growing up.

As mentioned previously, I was a very mediocre student. Was it because I didn't study hard enough? Nope. I had incredible study habits. I was just one of those students who needed to hear something multiple times in numerous different ways to fully understand what was being said. I look back and think, "Wow. Teachers must have hated me. I was so much work." It's true. It took a lot for me to comprehend things growing up.

However, I was motivated to understand what I was learning and do well at it. I suppose teachers respected me for that. One of my favorite teachers taught a class where I didn't perform well. I loved her because she was patient with me. She would meet with me during her lunch hour to tutor me and give me extra attention so I could do well. The feeling of finally understanding a concept was so rewarding.

When I was in university for elementary education, I learned that I needed to teach a concept in three ways to hit the diverse learners in my classroom. For example, I needed to get my point across audibly, visually, and kinesthetically. Even then, some students still would not understand.

Patience is everything! Especially when you deal with multiple personalities. Because I needed the extra help and patience from my teachers in school, I knew how other students felt when they just didn't get it. I never got mad or frustrated. I signed up to teach students step-by-step. I signed up to repeat myself five times before the point has been made. When a student finally understands, it is the most rewarding feeling in the world. It's like watching a child walk for the first time. It is simply amazing.

How does patience relate to Network Marketing and why do you NEED to have it if you want to be successful? Let's go over three aspects of the industry: sales, booking events, and recruiting.

Sales

Let's get one thing out of the way: We are NOT salespeople. We are in the business of sharing an incredible product and/or service.

We are in the business of sharing an incredible product and/or service.

"Selling" is simply the result of sharing, suggesting, and being of service to others. If you do not ask your customer what issue they need solved, how will you know what to recommend? Basically, if you do not have enough information on the person interested in purchasing what you have to offer, you will not be well equipped to give an adequate suggestion.

We truly are in the business of service. Being patient is an important customer service skill. We are not trying to rush people out the door. We are trying to satisfy our customers in the best way possible.

When a customer approaches you asking about your product and/or service, the goal is to find out as much as possible. Some questions you may ask are:

1. What is it that you are hoping to achieve? (It may be mental, physical, or emotional.)

2. How do you think this product/service could help you achieve that?

3. Have you tried anything in the past? Did it work?

4. Do you have any questions or concerns about this product/service?

Asking these key questions to a customer is important because you will be able to determine if your customer will be a good fit (or not) for this product. If you skip over this process, you could be left with an unhappy customer who will not return.

Show that you truly care about your customers' wants and needs. People are emotional beings. If you complete that sale knowing you did everything you could to recommend the right product rather than rush them out the door as soon as possible, they will remember you. They will be a returning customer and they will recommend you to others. When you come from a point of service and have that extra ounce of patience, you will maintain a thriving business.

Booking Events

Being part of a company that offers online or in-home presentations is a great way to expand your network. If you want to grow a team and be successful, you must meet new people. But what happens if you don't have patience in this process?

Do not go into a conversation with the sole intent of asking someone to host an event for you. Network Marketing is a relationship-building business. Go into conversations with no intent other than to be of service, and everything starts to change. It's a completely different conversation.

Many people give up on Network Marketing because they "cannot get any sales or book any events." But here's the truth: they can get sales and book the event, but that is what every conversation of theirs revolves around. They don't see the value in their opportunity.

Some companies have perks for holding an event. Why are we positioning holding or attending an event as something that benefits us, when we should be promoting the value that it can offer them. People want to know, "What is in it for me?" Tell them why they will benefit from booking an event with you. There are too many issues when you jump right into a conversation and the first message you send to someone is asking them to host an event with you.

1. It may not be the time to ask. Begin a conversation by asking someone how they are doing. What if something traumatic has recently happened? It probably is not the best time to ask them to book anything with you.

2. It's spammy. Spam is when you give someone information they never asked for. If you start a conversation telling someone why they need to do business with you, it will rub people the wrong way.

3. You're being selfish. Think more about what is in it for them. Think about how it could benefit them.

4. Have patience.

Here is a bad example versus a good example:

Bad Example

You: Hey Sally! How's it going? Hope you're doing well! I wanted to see how you've been enjoying your products? Also, have you considered hosting an event for me? They're fun and you could earn free and discounted products! What do you think?

Them: *Ignores*

Why It's Bad

If it's not obvious, there is way too much going on in that conversation. Not only is it a one-way conversation since you really don't give them any room to reply, but it just comes off as selfish and demonstrates poor customer service. Sally does not feel like you really care about her. Sally thinks that your only intent of messaging her was to book an event. It probably was.

Good Example

You: Hey Sally! How are you doing today?

Them: I'm doing well, how are you?

You: I'm glad to hear that! I'm well too! What have you been up to lately?

Them: Oh, I've been keeping busy with work, and yourself?

You: That's good to hear! I've been busy as well with my kids, business...etc. I'm actually messaging you as part of my customer care to check in on how you've been enjoying your new products?

Them: Awesome! Thanks for checking in. Everything has been great! I'm loving the _____. I also have a question about _____.

You: I'm glad to hear that you're enjoying it all! I would be more than happy to answer your question! (Answer question).

Them: Great, thanks so much!

You: No worries! Since you've been enjoying everything, I was wondering if you have ever considered hosting your own event so you can get more items on your wish list at a sweet deal! Does this sound like something you may be interested in?

Them: I would definitely consider it! What's involved?

...CONTINUES...

Why It's Good

Do you see why this conversation is much more effective?

First and foremost, you show interest in *them.* You show that you care. It's an actual conversation because you go back and forth with questions. You come from a point of service by doing customer care. You answer questions. Lastly, you suggest an event since they have been loving their products or services. This is just one example of a quality conversation that you can have when booking events.

Having patience makes the *biggest* difference in conversations. Have higher quality conversations, and you will develop a quality business.

Recruiting

Recruiting doesn't happen in seconds, minutes, hours, or even days. Patience is your best friend in building a sustainable team. Like

Patience is your best friend in building a sustainable team.

bookings, your goal is to have higher quality conversations with people.

However, the difference is that there is often an investment involved in joining a company. This can make the decision for the other person difficult. You may need to give them more time to think about it.

Rather than repeating most of the things I just said, go back and re-read the "Bookings" section, but look at it from a recruiting perspective.

I will give you some key questions you should ask someone considering your business opportunity and the mindset that you need to have around recruiting moving forward.

When someone approaches you asking about your business opportunity, your goal is to find out as much as possible about them and their goals. Some questions you may ask are:

1. What has interested you the most about this business opportunity?

2. What are you hoping to achieve from this opportunity? (Short-Term & Long-Term)

3. What are your expectations?

4. How much time do you have to put into this?

5. Do you have any questions or concerns about this opportunity?

Asking these key questions are important because you can determine if they are a good fit or not. If you skip over this process, you may end up with someone who has false expectations of what it takes to be successful— however that may look to them.

The point is that you should truly care about their goals and ensure they have a good understanding of what is expected of them to achieve that. Paint a clear picture for them. The more you genuinely care, the more they will care about their customers and potential recruits in the future. That is what will make you duplicatable and a memorable leader to them.

When you come from a point of service and have that extra ounce of patience, you will soar in this business, and grow a sustainable team!

Mindset Around Recruiting

You are offering an incredible opportunity — one that you were offered by someone else. If you don't believe that what you have to offer is incredible, you are not in the right mindset. Shift that mindset from "they're doing me a favor by joining my team" to "you are doing them a favor by offering them an opportunity with numerous benefits." Find out what that "thing" is that they need more of, and solve their problem.

The goal is to have better quality conversations every day. Have patience in everything you do.

You tell me what is better: a "no" that took one second or a "yes" that took one week? The "No's" grow you, but the "Yes's" grow your business. You want both. You do not grow without "no's." If you get zero "no's," you also get zero "yes's."

Dracy: Insecurities Packaged

"I have just three things to teach:
simplicity, patience, and compassion.
These three are your greatest treasures."
— *Lao Tzu*

Alison R, a blogger for Code of Living, wrote "7 Simple Tips to Become a More Patient Person." She said, "The coping style which you learned as a child is generally the same in later life. If you learned that kicking and screaming loudly resulted in your mom and dad caving in and letting you 'have it' you likely began with an initial low level of patience."

"On the other hand, if your mom or dad were firm but encouraging, you likely developed a different mindset when faced with inconveniences and likely began with a higher level of patience. As you grew older and progressed in life, your interactions with people defined the patience that you now have."

My nature is not patient. I wasn't brought up with firm and encouraging parenting. I was raised mostly by my grandmother in a home of many foster children. As much as I was loved, and with good intentions in my upbringing, time invested into developing coping skills was not one of them. I also learned that lack of patience is just "insecurities packaged."

When I succeeded in this industry, personal development was a side effect. I learned that if I wanted to become the highest-level leader with the company, I would have to study the art of patience.

John Maxwell has an incredible book "Laws of Leadership. " He stated patience as the most important quality. I realized, this was the top quality I had to nurture— not just in business, but in relationships, and myself. I am proud of this quality that I carry, in how I handle difficult situations and achieve the things I have achieved.

The first step into patience: realize it goes hand-in-hand with listening skills and a positive attitude. If you don't have those skills yet, you can't learn patience without developing them. Patience also kicks in persistence. It is an art that doesn't happen overnight and so you need to persevere.

There were five areas I needed to practice patience:

1. Adapting to change

2. Learning something new

3. Other people learning new skills

4. Decision making

5. Achieving goals

Know what triggers your impatience. Prepare and visualize the results you desire. Impatience can mean pent-up stress, tension, anxiety, lack of support or just not knowing what to do. Being tired, not looking after yourself all can be factors in not coping. Even deep-rooted insecurities or other people. You have control over all these things.

Tips to Become More Patient

1. Practice Gratitude: This to be the most important ingredient— daily gratitude. This practice highly rewards you as a human and all accomplishments.

2. Love the Process: This eliminates pressure. Life and people become more enjoyable.

3. Be Self-Confident: Patience and confidence go hand-in-hand. Confidence is the decision to be brave and practice, practice, practice.

4. Visualize Your Outcomes: Who is the person you want to become? Set yourself up with visualizing. Record the person you want to become. Describe every situation and circumstance and visualize how you would like to respond vs react. The more you practice this, the more you will become.

5. Find Support: A coach is extremely important.

6. Read: My best teachers on this topic were John Maxwell and Jim Rohn.

7. Follow Simple Systems: Onboard new recruits and be a leader. You need a *simple* system.

No matter your background or upbringing, you can do great things and make a difference. The most important person you need to be patient with is *yourself.*

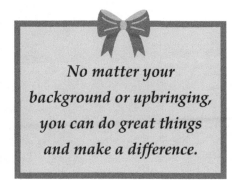

No matter your background or upbringing, you can do great things and make a difference.

By doing this, the rewards are: better relationships, less stress (overwhelm), your productivity over time will increase, and you will become better at teaching. By becoming better at teaching, you will create leaders. By creating leaders in this industry you will become respected, admired and successful.

"Wanting to win is not enough,
you have to go through the process to improve.
That takes patience, perseverance and intentionality."
— *John Maxwell*

"In any situation you can think of,
impatience is a source of weakness and fear,
while patience represents substance and strength.
— *Jim Rohn*

Chapter 5: The Gift of Focus

Teisha: Your Confident "Why"

The best way to gain focus in your business is to find your "why." For example, many people who have kids, pets or loved ones focus on giving them a quality life. They focus on their health, happiness, and more. When you run a business with the intent of creating a quality life for you and your loved ones, the one thing that will keep you focused is your "why."

Business is not always smooth sailing. You will have good and bad seasons. One thing that will remain consistent is your "why." Whatever your end goal is, make sure that every action you take brings you one step closer to that end goal.

When I started my Network Marketing journey, I had no intent of going big. In fact, I didn't think it was possible for me. However, I had focus. It was something I loved to do— it was healthy for my mind, heart, and body. When you are so obsessed with something that makes you a better person all around, why would you ever stop doing that thing? I focused on the only thing I knew: my love and belief for my products. My passion helped me grow and took me to where I am today.

Focus on the new and the exciting in your business. When you get excited about something, other people will get excited with you too. Your audience will never be more excited than you are.

If you focus on the challenges and the negative "what-ifs" running through your head daily, it affects your mood and 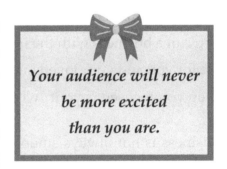 excitement in your business. Your audience recognizes that emotion and form doubts.

Your audience will never be more excited than you are.

Example: if your family doctor wasn't confident they were good at their job, would you choose them as your family doctor? Or look for someone else? I'm assuming you would look for someone else.

In your business, if you're confident in what you do and offer, others will be too. Focus on the exciting parts of what you do, and the reason why you do what you do. Share it often and growth will follow.

Increased Focus

Here are three factors I've changed in my life to increase focus:

1. My circle of family and friends. Let's be honest, family and friends can be stressful once in a while. It's normal. But the biggest red flag is when they're not there for the important things in your life. Do they clap for you when you succeed? Or do they turn the other way and show jealousy? Your circle, whether there are 2 or 20 people in it, should be there for you through the good and bad. I promise that life hits different when you cut out toxic people.

2. A morning routine. Working from home and for yourself has its perks and challenges. Although I have the liberty to work when I want, it can be a curse at times. A routine helps start my day with good energy and intention. I wake up early and work out for 30 minutes. Then, I physically get ready for the day. I would love to work in my pajamas every day, but I don't feel as productive or ready when I do that. I put nice clothes on, do my hair, and makeup, to set the mood for my day. It motivates me to do more.

Next, I spend 15 minutes making my to-do list for the day and prioritizing tasks. Then, I read personal or professional development for 15 minutes, network on my socials for 30 minutes, and tackle my to-do list for the day. This ensures I get the most important things out of the way in the morning, leaving the afternoon more open to accomplishing larger long-term goals.

3. Set business hours. I never saw the value in setting business hours until my relationships and business suffered. If you're a leader in your business trying to make this work for you and your family, set business hours. If you don't respect your time and personal life, neither will anyone else. If you're doing this to achieve time freedom, set a good example with your team. Promoting the business as a way to find "time freedom" but not actually having that freedom in your own life is hypocritical. You deserve the life that you want to have.

Customers and teammates can wait for their questions to be answered. If anything, setting business hours makes you more duplicatable in your business and helps you grow more sustainable leaders on your team. You can implement this now or learn the hard way, like I did. I'd suggest now.

Self-Actualization, Esteem, Love, Safety & Physiological Needs

Maslow's Hierarchy of Needs is a concept I often visit when I don't feel I'm performing at my best. I actually wrote a 30+ page report on this concept years ago and how it related to at-risk students. However, this hierarchy relates to several aspects of life, including your focus and performance in network marketing.

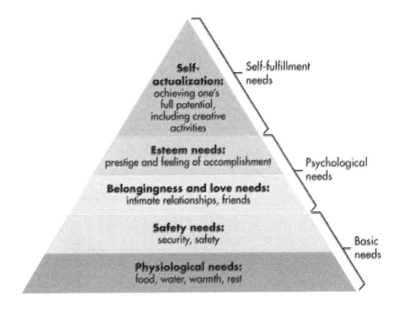

As explained by SimplePsychology.org (2020), "Maslow's hierarchy of needs is a motivational theory in psychology comprising a five-tier model of human needs, often depicted as hierarchical levels within a pyramid. From the bottom of the hierarchy upwards, the needs are: physiological (food and clothing), safety (job security), love and belonging needs (friendship), esteem, and self-actualization. Needs lower down in the hierarchy must be satisfied before individuals can attend to needs higher up."

Physiological needs are your most basic needs. For example, physiological needs include your health, the type and amount of food you consume, and your sleep habits. Safety needs include your shelter and removal from danger. Love and belonging needs: the love and affection you receive from others and your groups. This is considered to be a psychological need. Your esteem level is also considered a psychological need — your self-esteem and esteem from others.

Lastly, self-actualization, a self-fulfillment need, is your ability to achieve individual potential. This theory has plenty to offer when it comes to explaining how you, as a Network Marketer, can and will achieve your full potential in this industry.

At times, why are you not achieving your full potential? Why do you not feel as accomplished as you would like to in your business? Numerous factors can weigh in as to why you're not reaching your goals, but it could be a sign you need to focus on your basic needs. If those aren't being met, it's difficult to achieve self-actualization.

For instance, have you ever tried reading and comprehending a book when you are physically exhausted? It simply does not work. Your brain does not function at a high enough capacity to learn anything when you don't get enough sleep at night. Personally, I find it difficult to get work done when I'm feeling tired or hungry, since those are the *only* things on my mind.

Many fall into the trap of their belonging and love needs not being met. Maintain good and strong relationships with your loved ones. Many people join Network Marketing for the community and fun. It can be difficult to put your phone or laptop down and stop working your business, especially in the evenings. However, you do more harm than good by not setting business hours for yourself. Ensure you get quality time with your significant other. Otherwise, this lack can affect your end result and hinder you from achieving your goals.

Ensure your basic and psychological needs are met, so you can move towards a more effective focus on your self-fulfillment needs, hit your goals and reach the full potential in your business to succeed. Don't allow the basics to slip through the cracks.

Dracy: Focused or Fried

If you don't find a way to be focused you will find yourself becoming fried, overwhelmed, and easily stressed.

Focus can be easy or it can be hard. Like eating an apple a day, easy to do and easy not to do. Interestingly, it brings to mind the word "discipline."

The rewards of focus are so great. It is literally achieving anything you put your mind to. Whatever goal you set for yourself requires this element.

However, today, more than ever before there are many distractions. Obvious distractions and subtle distractions.

Obvious, being online distraction, social media, checking email, watching television, or playing games on our phone. The battle plays out in front of you each day.

"Subtle" is even more destructive because it can take residence in your heart and paralyze you from what really matters.

Five Steps to Focus

Step 1: Recognize the Distractions

"Starve your distractions, feed your focus."
— *Anonymous*

An article "9 Ever Present Distractions That Keeps Us From Fully Living" written by Joshua Becker, author of "Minimalist Home, The More of Less, and Things that Matter" gave me insight to my awareness, making me better equipped to focus towards my goals using these tools:

1. The Promise of Tomorrow. Joshua Glenn Clark said, "We waste so many days waiting for the weekend. Many nights wanting morning. Our lust for future comfort is the biggest thief of life." It is not entirely foolish to look toward the future and plan accordingly. However, when you endure your days only for the sake of tomorrow (the weekend, the vacation, or retirement), you miss out on the full beauty and potential of the present.

2. The Pursuit of Perfection. Pursue excellence and pride in all you do. Your next step forward should be the right next step, taken with as much intention as possible. However, doing your best and achieving perfection are rarely the same. When perfection becomes the goal, it becomes the enemy of progress—this distracts you from taking the essential risk of moving forward.

3. The Regret of Yesterday. To live is to experience regret. Nobody escapes life unscathed. We all regret our actions, decisions, and motivations. However, no amount of regret can change the past. Only those who have come to recognize and admit their imperfections are able to move beyond them. Call your mistakes what they are, offer an apology when necessary, and move on. Don't allow regret from the past to negatively distract from opportunity in the present.

4. The Accumulation of Possessions. Things you own require time, energy, money, and attention. Every increased possession adds increased stress in your life. Yet, you continue to pursue and accumulate more and more and more. More is not the answer. "More" has become the distraction.

5. The Desire for Wealth. Those who chase riches have misplaced their greatest potential and traded it to the highest bidder. Your life was designed for contribution— to provide a positive impact on society for yourself, your family, and those who live in your community. Sometimes, contribution provides financial excess. Other times, it does not. Either way, when your contribution to society becomes chiefly motivated by a selfish desire to accumulate riches, it has become self-focused. You have lost your opportunity to live it to the fullest.

6. The Need for Notoriety. The life you live is the life you live, regardless if anybody notices or not. Those who live lives focused on the need to be recognized are usually the first to take shortcuts to get there. Instead, find significance in the eyes of those who know you best— that is all that matters, anyway.

7. The Pull of Comparison. By nature, you feel compelled to compare your life to those around you. It's easy to compare your belongings, appearance, families, and successes. Every time you do, you place your focus and energy on the wrong person. Comparing yourself to others causes you to regret what you are not, rather than allowing you to enjoy and grow who you are.

8. The Appeal of Pleasure. Are you led astray by the appeal and pursuit of pleasure? You might ask, "Why not? What is wrong with the pursuit of pleasure?"

Pleasure is a terrible teacher. The most significant lessons you learn in life are rarely received during times of pleasure. They are born out of pain. Do not seek pain in your life. However, be aware that a life lived chiefly for the pursuit of pleasure, will seek it in the wrong places.

9. The Presence of Indifference. The world is a big place— you have much to offer. If you choose to live life as a victim, you will miss your opportunity to give. If you choose to adopt an indifference to the world, you will miss out on your greatest potential. Recognize "need"— seek to do something about it, in order to experience a joy and fulfillment that can never be discovered anywhere else.

The world is full of distraction—the most dangerous are those you do not recognize.

Step 2: Create a Clear Picture of What You Want

"The direction of your focus
is the direction your life will move.
Let yourself move towards what is good,
valuable, strong and true."
— Ralph Marston

Write down your goals and dreams. Make a vision board. Why do you want this in your life? Know the difference it will make in your life and the lives around you. Creating a fire in your belly that burns, that gets you excited so that you jump out of bed and greet the dawn with enthusiasm and be satisfied at dusk, knowing you have done the activities it takes to achieve them, whilst enjoying the process brings great satisfaction.

The first book I read, on my self development journey, was about Creative Visualization.

I crafted the life I wanted as if it had already happened. I remember building my first dream chart, illustrating what I wanted to do, be, and have.

Just recently, my 21-year-old son created a dream chart as part of my date night with them on financial literacy. The joy and enthusiasm that it brought to their hearts reminded me of the dream charts I created over the years.

When I drew my second dream chart I did, I was recently married. I was in the process of success, achieving great things, and accomplishing everything on my first chart, which was relatively conservative. The second chart was huge, the size of four poster board billboards. I had the word "baby" written on it three times. Then, I gave birth to three babies in two and a half years. I laugh about this to this day.

I drew waterfront property, 400 acres in Australia, boats, BMW's, dogs. You name it, it was there. By 33, I had achieved those things. What was important was the person I became in the process. It wasn't just about "things" on my chart— there were qualities of the person I needed to become to achieve them. Disciplined, focused, hard working, patience, and supportive community.

This process becomes your autoplot.

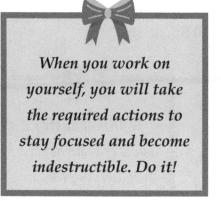

When you work on yourself, you will take the required actions to stay focused and become indestructible. Do it!

When you cannot determine what is real or not, program it like it has already happened, with pictures, consciously visualizing, writing, sharing and talking about your goals and dreams. When you work on yourself, you will take the required actions to stay focused and become indestructible. *Do it!*

Step 3: Create a Road Map

Follow One Course Until Successful.

In this industry, success is measured by helping other people achieve and move up the leadership ranks. Robert Kiyosaki, known for "Rich Dad Poor Dad," is an advocate for network marketing; he even wrote a book

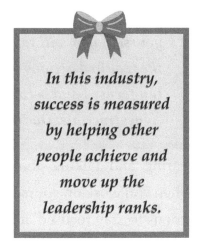

In this industry, success is measured by helping other people achieve and move up the leadership ranks.

about it called "The Business of the 21 Century." The book recommends you give Network Marketing a shot and commit for at least five years. After five years, if you give it your all, you will be wealthier, have more freedom, more control of your life, and become a better person.

When Donald Trump was asked on TV and shared on the internet, what he was going to do if he was to go bankrupt once again, his answer was simple. He said that he would get into a network marketing business.

The industry is favored by its business plan. It is not favored by those unwilling to put in the work on themselves. The industry has a proven track record.

Your company should have a proven track record and a roadmap attached to each level of leadership. Each level of leadership has an average income. Work out your income goal, find out what level of leadership that is attached to it, and get to work. Better yet, if you already have team members, help them work out their income goals, then what level of leadership is required, and get to work together.

I attended my first conference with new and raw enthusiasm. I saw the beautiful rewards, paycheques, flowers and pretty dresses. I made a decision that that was going to be me next year. I was new, had just started and by the next year's conference I was at the highest level of the company on stage, receiving all those rewards. That is what I visualized every day. I was given a roadmap of activities, how many people I needed and how many leaders I needed to create and support to achieve this dream.

I remember my upline, taking me to the office supplies and buying labels, poster board, black markers and highlighters. On the way to the store, she asked me what type of new car I wanted, what color, and we stopped at the car dealer to pick up the brochure. Once we had the supplies, we created a roadmap and tracking sheet to achieve the first level of leadership. If I performed that same process with any willing participant, I would achieve my goals. Each label represented a person. The person's name was written on the label, what was required of them, and what daily activities were needed from me. A team name and a date. This roadmap is impregnated in my brain, and anyone who has worked with me would have created one, as well as a dream chart.

Step 4: Get a Coach

"When you focus on the problems,
you have more problems.
When you focus on possibilities,
you have more opportunities."
— Zig Ziglar

A coach or upline will help you stay focused on this outcome. That is why you want a coach that is living the life you desire, has done the work, knows  *The right coach wants for you, not from you.* what needs to be done, and keeps you accountable and focused— someone that shares your enthusiasm, helping you through struggles and challenges.

The right coach wants *for* you, not *from* you. They are honest and will tell you what you *need* to hear, not what you *want* to hear.

Step 5: Time Management

"Time that leads to mastery is
dependent on the intensity of your focus."
— Robert Greene

Become an expert. This is a skill that can be learned. The better you become at it, the faster and more successes you will achieve with ease. Run your business based on the metaphor of the "big rocks and the sand." Schedule the most important activities, personally and professionally. Mark your calendars with highlighters three months in advance, and break your days into a three-part day.

Highlight your date nights, holidays, and weekends off. Become disciplined using your time for revenue generating activities. This process helps with your boundaries on what you can and can't do. You will make better choices on the people you spend your time with.

The times in my life that I have not implemented this were the times I lost my focus and was easily distractible. Anyone can be busy, but are you busy doing the right things that help you become a better person? It's important to

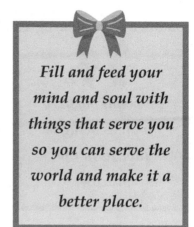

Fill and feed your mind and soul with things that serve you so you can serve the world and make it a better place.

fill and feed your mind and soul with things that serve you so you can serve the world and make it a better place. You can always ask a procrastinator what they are watching or reading— it will always be a fictional book, or Netflix. Ask someone who is focused and they will tell you about the self-development book or program they are reading or listening to.

You are a work in progress. Personal mastery involves being in love with the process. Find joy in what you do, and focus becomes easy and fun. You can't even hear the noisy dump truck outside or the planes overhead when you are focused.

Personal mastery involves being in love with the process.

> *"Focus like a laser, not a flashlight."*
> — *Michael Jordan*

P.S. To write these chapters, I've had to turn my phone off and no Facebook tab on my computer.

Chapter 6: The Gift of Community

Teisha: Build a Community with Your Customers

The main reason people *start* a Network Marketing business is to make extra income. The main reason people *stay* in the industry is because of the community. Building community in your business helps you grow. But what does it mean to "build community?" You will build a community with your customers. You will create a community with your team. You can utilize the community already established by your company.

Several distributors create a private group, (sometimes known as an online community or a VIP group) when starting their business. The intent of this group may be looked at differently by each person. For instance, many people will use the private customer group to share what's new, show the latest promotions and offers, and display product profiles. However, others may use the group for the above and also share their own personal journey with their business and products. Some people use their group for all of the above *plus* encourage engagement and success stories of others within the group.

There is no right or wrong way to run your group. Everyone has a different intent and goal when starting in a Network Marketing company. It may be to purchase products for themselves. It may be to share with close friends and family. It may be to make a part-time income. It may be to make a full-time income, or make an uncapped income. Whatever it is depends on the intent of your private customer group.

However, if you're reading this book, it's because you want to level up in your business— maybe even "see where it takes you." That's how many think when they start a side business like this. The bottom line is: those with the *most* successful businesses are those who create that aspect of community within their private groups.

When I started with my current company (which is also my only network marketing company experience), I did what anyone else would do if they were new and had no idea what to post: stock photos of the products, sharing features of the products, relaying information I read through the consultant groups. There are thousands, or even millions of people doing the *exact* same thing that you are. How will you stand out? Everyone has access to the stock photos, the features, and the information you learn about the products. However, no one else has your story. Why do you do what you do? How has your product or service impacted you? How has it impacted your customers? Are you asking your customers for their feedback?

Example

Person 1: Look at this weight loss product. It will help you lose weight because of ingredients X, Y, and Z. It comes in a bottle that looks like this. This is how you take it. Who wants to try some?

Person 2: This weight loss product has impacted me and dozens of my customers! I used to look and feel like this and now I feel like that after using it for x amount of time. My customer Sally struggled with this and started using the product. Look at her results now! Who needs some?

Who would you have more trust in? Person, 1 selling the features and benefits? Or Person 2, sharing their story and customer testimonials? My guess is that your answer is Person 2, considering you can trust that the product has actually worked on people you know.

The point I'm trying to make is that facts tell, and stories sell. If you want a successful and flourishing business, you must be personable and relatable with your customers. Share your own personal story and journey, as well as the stories of others that your product or service has impacted. Doing this through a private customer group is the perfect way to create community and build trust with your customers. Invite them into a safe space where they can share freely, how they're enjoying their products and/or services you've provided them with.

Here are my top tips for creating community in your private group:

- Go live often (live demonstrations, introduce yourself, Q&A)
- Ask for opinions (regarding your product and random life situations)
- Invite them to share (ask them questions in your posts)
- Reward them for sharing (giveaways)

- Welcome new members (keep it exciting, new and welcoming)
- Offer special promotions just for them (discounts, special offers)
- Create a schedule and share it with them (Motivation Monday - share a quote, Transformation Tuesday - share a customer testimonial, Wednesday Wisdom - share a tip, Throwback Thursday - share a good memory, Freebie Friday - do a giveaway!)
- Post 1-2 engagement posts per week (question of the week, fill in the blank, trivia, polls - something that invites people to comment & get involved)

The more you encourage your customers to participate in your group, the more active it will be and the more curiosity you will create. Every single day, think to yourself, "How will I create curiosity today?" Curiosity leads to questions. Questions lead you to resolving your customers' problems through your products and services.

Team Community

The most exciting part about leadership is the team you build, and the people you impact. Once you build your team, it's easy to forget what you went through when you first started. Depending on the type of person and experience they have, there may be some hand-holding. Don't make the mistake of neglecting your newbies. Recruiting can be a difficult task, especially if you've never done it before. When you finally get that first person to join your team, you feel proud of yourself— it is like the task is over and done with.

Mission accomplished? Not quite. It's the opposite. Just like a teacher or a parental figure, teaching your lesson does not mean that you are finished. You have to make sure that the lesson was understood. A baby doesn't learn how to walk when you tell it how to walk. It learns by repetition, practice, and guidance. It's the same with starting a new business.

Do you remember what I said earlier was the main reason people join, versus why they stay in Network Marketing? That's right, it's the community. If you neglect your newbies, they will not feel a sense of community or belonging. Establish that through your team group you've created specifically for your teammates. You will have meetings, recognize accomplishments, deliver quality training, and get to know one another.

My team is a tight-knit crew because of the community that has been created within my team group. I wasn't great at this when I initially started. Balancing my own business with my team was a struggle. I tend to be a perfectionist and like things done my way. This put extra work on my hands, and took away from the many opportunities to involve my team in events and projects. After changing my ways, I let go of the "perfectionism" mindset— I created an incredible team and community of people who I call some of my closest friends today.

That "aha moment" was when someone asked me if I was duplicatable. They asked if anyone on my team could see themselves in the same position I was in my own business. I realized that I was in fact not duplicatable. I was reinventing the wheel, creating graphics, and providing *everything* I've ever created. I've always loved to share creation with my team, but I never included my team in projects. I never showed them the effort. I never thought to consider that someone else might be good at this. When I handed out more opportunities, we grew closer together.

You are a part of something *much bigger* than just a company selling good products or offering some quality services. You are a part of a community who has your back.

To create community with your team:

- Let them help you with team projects (graphics or planning)
- Give them a role during your team events (posting, live videos, training tips...etc.)
- Shout them out for something they rock at and ask them to deliver a training for the team
- Have team meetings for recognition and upcoming events
- Host team opportunity events to build others
- Host an in-person team get together if possible (if not, do it through Zoom)
- Create group chats with 5-10 people working on the same goal or are at a similar level in their business. Keep each other accountable. You'll see their relationships grow.
- Ask for their opinions on literally ANYTHING!

When you get a group of people excited about the same thing and continue to show them the potential that they have within them, they will flourish. Their energies will bounce off one another and create a movement within their business.

Utilize the already established community by your company.

When you started in your Network Marketing business, you were likely invited to join a group that included all of the distributors within the company. Each company runs their group differently, but a common goal is to create community in that space. A place for you to ask questions, get suggestions, and learn more.

It's important to get to know others outside of your team as well. I personally have a wonderful group of leaders, outside of my team that I talk to on a daily basis. These are people who I've met at Leadership Summits or online through mutual leader friends. These are the people at the same stage as me in my business.

People who understand the wins and the daily struggles leaders go through. These are my people.

They keep me motivated, sane, and we share many ideas and resources. If your team has in-person events, go! Meet new people and build your own smaller community within the company that is already established. It's so easy to build relationships with people who already have something in common with you. These company conferences and summits will help you take your business to new levels.

Never stop expanding your circle.

Community is everything — I can't express that enough. Stop focusing on how you can make money and start focusing on how to impact others and build your community. The results will follow. Make it a goal to grow your community's team, customers, and business allies every day. The more people you communicate with and build stronger connections with, the more successful you will be. Never stop expanding your circle.

"Your network is your net worth."
— Porter Gale

Dracy: Unwrap the Leader in You

"Community is where humility and glory touch."
— *Henri J.M. Nouwen*

Network Marketing is a community. A community creates a space for you to grow and feel safe. You enter the community because you have a common passion. You are humble because you are new, unknowing, looking for a sense of direction and inspiration. Then, you become that inspiration and the one giving direction. The glory is in overcoming the challenges and achievements through the community and connection.

No one is alone. The success is in helping everyone equally step up. All one has to do is show up. In the right community, you can stand out, then create your own community by repeating the process of humility, and celebrating the glory together.

There are two positions in a community: a participant and a leader. Your ultimate goal is to help people lead their own groups and create their own communities.

To do that, you must learn to be a great participant. Show up, share, support, step up, and say "yes" to challenges.

Your group must be led by a great leader, who is humble and shares the glory.

Like an infinity symbol, a community is ever growing. The symbol for infinity is ∞. Initially called the Lemniscate, meaning "ribbon," by the ancient Greek, the infinity sign carries the shape of a sideways figure eight, a twisted ribbon that has no beginning or end. Start tracing from any point on the infinity symbol "ribbon" and you will never reach an "end" but will continue on the infinity loop forever.

As we unwrap the leader in you, your community is the ribbon. This is where the magic comes. The glory in watching them grow and unwrap their gifts. Like the ribbon, it becomes infinite. It is the bow on your gift.

12 Steps to a Great Community

Think of 8 ways to make each step MAGIC.

1. Collabor8
2. Cultiv8
3. Communic8
4. Cre8
5. Evalu8
6. Activ8
7. Particip8
8. Motiv8
9. Appreci8
10. Toler8
11. Navig8
12. Illumin8

EXAMPLE: 1. What are 8 idea's you can do to get your community to Collabor8 more? This is a powerful exercise to continually grow infinite.

> *"Only in a community with others*
> *does each individual have the means*
> *to cultivate their gifts in all directions.*
> *Only in a community therefore,*
> *is personal freedom possible."*
> — *Karl Marx*

131

Chapter 7: The Gift of Passion & Purpose

Teisha: Take Risks

*"A true passion that burns within your soul
is one that can never be put out."*
— *Zach Toelke*

My favorite people in this world are those with so much passion and love for what they do. Have you been in contact with someone working their job who hates what they're doing? We all have. It may be someone at the front desk, a cashier, a waiter, a teacher, or a mechanic. Whatever occupation, some people are just better off doing something else. Nothing grinds my gears more than having a conversation with someone who doesn't want to be doing what they're doing. It's a terrible experience for everyone:

1. The **worker** because they're clearly having a bad day or hates what they're doing in general.

2. The **customer** because they never deserved that kind of negative energy.

Passion goes much further than skills ever will.

I'm walking proof of that. Pursue what you love, because if you do what you love, you'll never work a day in your life! Plus, who doesn't want to get paid to do what they love?

I attended university, graduating with an elementary education degree and a psychology degree. It wasn't my passion to teach children.

Passion goes much further than skills ever will.

I was great at it considering my creative abilities and love for planning. However, I could tell that my career as a teacher would be short-lived. I never had the love for it as much as others did.

I was introduced to the Network Marketing industry and found my true passion. It began with a product, but resulted in a full-time career of leading and helping others. I never attended university for business. The idea of having a business and working for myself never seemed doable for someone like me at the time.

Being naturally shy and preferring to keep to myself most of the time didn't seem like the qualities someone should have when going into a business or sales position. However, I was completely wrong. At first, I thought my passion was for the products, which I love, but my deeper purpose was helping others and being of service. My purpose was to lead. Deep down, I always had those leadership qualities and they just needed to be unwrapped. My mentor and co-author Dracy supported me in this new role, and that's how my passion for leadership bloomed.

I knew teaching wouldn't be my be-all end-all. I chose it so spontaneously and never felt fulfilled during my university years. I was afraid I would never find something I was deeply passionate about. I am grateful and fortunate Dracy was persistent with me, hearing out what the opportunity entailed. If it wasn't for her, I wouldn't have discovered my biggest burning passion in life.

Today, I know how important it is to share a business opportunity with others. It's selfish to keep it to yourself. It could make the biggest difference in someone's life. If you're not the one to share it, it's only a matter of time until someone else does. My life has made a complete 180 since diving into this industry full-time. I knew I had found my passion when I was more confident and happier in doing what I loved. It was an indescribable feeling. (You just know it's your path when you discover the right one.)

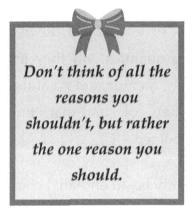

Don't think of all the reasons you shouldn't, but rather the one reason you should.

If you do not feel fulfilled in what you're doing, continue to try, learn, and take risks. Don't think of all the reasons you shouldn't, but rather the one reason you should.

A positive mindset combined with a good attitude is what will help you get to where you want to be today. You are given one life— don't waste it thinking, "What if I would have tried that?"

Just try it! You have nothing to lose. In fact, you have *so much* to gain! If someone were to hand me a billion dollars today, I still would not stop doing what I'm doing, because that is how powerful my purpose is. It's a part of me now. I continue to be a lifelong learner and discover new sub passions that support me in my bigger purpose.

I love to lead. I love social media marketing. I love to create graphics. I love to help others discover their confidence. I have many passions that support my bigger purpose, to serve others. Your passions may not excite you every single day— you are a human with feelings and you don't always feel motivated. However, when you recognize your bigger purpose and find a way to energize yourself in a new way, perhaps through a different passion, your dreams will continue to come true. Don't limit yourself by thinking you need to be a high achiever in order to be successful. Consider being a wide achiever an accomplishment as well. It means you're flexible, adaptable, and portray various skills. Find a reason to get excited every day. Never stop discovering who you are.

7 Signs You Haven't Yet Found Your Purpose or Passions

- You dread going to work
- You are unhappy in general
- You feel like you're not getting paid enough for what you do
- It's hard to get back up after a setback
- You're constantly checking the time to see when you're done for the day
- You don't feel proud to share what you do

137

- You constantly question why you're doing what you're doing

5 Steps to Finding Your Passions & Making It Your Job

- **Identify which skills you excel at and which ones you'd like to have and use.** Teamwork, leadership, analyzing data, problem solving, music.
- **Identify what you'd like to get out of your work**. Making a difference, having a positive impact, experiencing variety, making money, self happiness.
- **Describe the type of work environment that would be the most ideal for you.** Dress up every day, commute to work, working outdoors, working from home, working from anywhere.
- **Try new things that align with the above points.** Give each job or hobby an honest shot. Go become the best at it. Invest in it. Take a course on it. Get a mentor.
- **Avoid negative energy.** Surround yourself with positive people who are uplifting and support you.

The world doesn't need any more copies or replicas. The world needs more leaders. It needs more people who are willing to step up and

The world doesn't need any more copies or replicas.

follow their dreams. It needs more people who will lead by example and show others that they can do *anything* they set their mind to. The world needs *you* to unwrap your gifts within!

Dracy: Burn, Baby, Burn!

"Light yourself on fire with passion,
people will come from miles to watch you burn."
— Jon Wesley

Humans are attracted to fire, as an attempt to get power. When you ooze fire from your passion, people are attracted to you.

This is an attraction business, and you want to be attractive. People can see your attractiveness beaming through you. You are eager to be present and share your

When you ooze fire from your passion, people are attracted to you.

light. When you have that light, you want everyone to have it. Share the products, share the opportunities because you love it so much and you know how it has impacted your life. Why wouldn't you want to share it? You would be selfish not to.

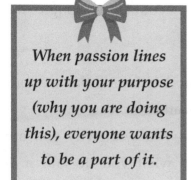

When passion lines up with your purpose (why you are doing this), everyone wants to be a part of it.

Passion makes you want to jump out of bed in the morning, charge, and make things happen. When passion lines up with your purpose (why you are doing this), everyone wants to be a part of it. They want what you have. Building your community, selling your position and product become easy.

Network marketing is an entrepreneur's dream. There are more people in the industry than ever before. It is only continuing to grow as more people lose their jobs, "have had enough" of being told what to do, or just not living their passion.

Passion is an emotion that translates to intense enthusiasm. Like yeast is to rising bread, enthusiasm is to growing a business. It gives you an eager interest in learning

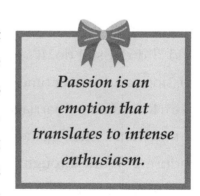

Passion is an emotion that translates to intense enthusiasm.

what you need to drive yourself through the challenges and difficult times.

Your purpose will make your decisions, influence your behaviors, shape your goals and give you the sense of direction you need to align you with why you are doing this. When you love what you do and it is aligned with your purpose, you have a longer, prosperous life.

In this business, you must be a product of the product, love people, be in love with personal growth, love the process, love learning new skills, love helping people achieve their goals and the love is going to flow your way. That usually translates into dollars. This is a paycheck of the heart.

Anyone who knows me, knows that I beam, I'm so in love with what I do. After almost 30 years when I first said "I do," I still do. It's just different. Your love and passions evolve over time. You can fall out of love, just like a love affair or marriage. The honeymoon stage has a timeframe, then something becomes lasting and enduring. Work through the hard times, finding new passions. This business is the same. There are many rewards, but there are also heartbreaking experiences. This business can beat you up. People start for one reason but stay for many other reasons. Yes, people will leave and remarry over and over. Jump from one company to another, till they find their match.

That is why it is important to know why you do this. Focus your passion. Work through the things that you don't like to do. Take breaks when you need to.

> ### Constantly re-evaluate your purpose and what this has done for your spirit, family and future.

You cannot fool people. Surround yourself with like minded people. Be in the pursuit of rising up and helping people. Have an upline or coach that is living life with purpose and passion to help you never lose your way.

> ### Get good at helping people find their passions and gifts, so they can shine and share those gifts.

Together, you all become a bush fire and can burn together.

Four Steps to Help Your Team Find Their Passion

1. Help Them Find Their Purpose. People want to be part of something bigger than themselves. Help them find that. What will drive them? Is it family, personal growth, recognition, money, being a part of a team, travel, or owning their own time?

2. Focus On Their Interests & Skills. We all naturally gravitate towards things we are interested in and are good at. They play a significant role in building our confidence and often form our passion.

3. Spend Quality Time With Them. This is the only way you can get to know them, learn what you need to, to help them and to let them experience *you*. That is why events, conventions, trips, adventures and coaching calls all play an important role.

4. Pay Attention. Get your team involved, people support what they help create. When you learn to delegate really well, it will be by paying attention to what your team is good at, and can match them with people and activities that will help them grow and shine. This will ignite or highlight their passions.

Chapter 8: The Gift of Action

Teisha: Income Producing Activities

As an entrepreneur and Network Marketer, you are in a relationship-building business. You thrive on making new connections and strengthening current ones. With the excitement you get making new friends, it can be easy to get distracted along the way.

For instance, you may be scrolling on a social media platform with the intent of networking with others through posts and stories. However, it's easy to get distracted by an attention-grabbing news article or a funny cat video.

You can get carried away by these distractions and "go down the rabbit hole" mid-day. First, you're just checking out some funny videos because you need a break, and then you find yourself scrolling for hours. It's all fun and games until you let your daily to-do list slip away and you cut into evening family time because you never finished the important tasks.

Being a millennial, on the verge of Gen Z's, social media can consume my life. I run my business through social media and can understand the struggle. It can be a blessing and a curse.

If your goal is to have a thriving business online, keep your head in the game. Focus on income producing activities  throughout the day. It's easy to feel busy, yet unproductive. Rinse and repeat the basics.

It's easy to feel busy, yet unproductive.

As a network marketing leader, the basics break down as follows: **Book, Sell, Recruit.**

If you can book online or in-home events, you can educate others on what you have to offer that can change their lives. If you can share your products and services, then you can impact others. And if you can impact others, you can share your opportunity and build your team. It's all easier said than done though, right? Smaller steps go into this process. To continue to have a thriving business, focus on the income producing activities.

I will share my daily, weekly, and monthly task schedules— to give you an idea of what to prioritize in your own business. It may also give you an idea of what tasks you could delete, delegate, or defer. If none of these options work, it could be a sign that you must DO the task. The 4 D's will help you organize your time better, so you have more time to focus on things that help your business grow.

The first step is to make a list of the tasks you do daily, weekly, & monthly. To figure out which of the 4 "D's" should be used for each task, follow the chart below:

- *Deleting* means it's not important for your growth
- *Delegating* means that someone else could take on this task, such as a team member or a virtual assistant
- *Deferring* means it's not something that is urgent RIGHT NOW
- *Doing* means you MUST do the task in order for you to grow in your business

The 4 D's of Time Management
Network Marketing Leadership Edition

Once you've figured out which tasks are non-negotiables, they can be added to your calendar, along with the rest of your income producing tasks that help you grow.

Daily

Each day, I follow a morning routine that ensures I get the most important tasks done at the beginning of the day for my personal business. These include important tasks AND my non-negotiables, including: working out, getting ready for the day, making my daily to-do list, and tackling it until lunch time. My income producing activities every morning within my routine include: reading 15 minutes of personal or professional development and intentional networking on my social platforms to make new connections.

Weekly

Every week, I have a short checklist of tasks to complete before the week is over. These tasks include: customer care by following up with people on their past orders and checking in with customers within my private community. This could be for a simple follow-up or to say hello and build stronger connections. I also like to ensure I'm checking in with different team members throughout the week. Another activity that helps grow my business is live videos. I try to do at least 1-2 per week in my private community and public page. Lastly, I plan for the upcoming week.

Monthly

Specific tasks I like to do throughout the month include: sharing my "why" with customers. I sprinkle this in weekly through social media posts, but it's important to share through live presentations too. I run a team opportunity event or call each month to set that recruiting atmosphere within my team. Do this consistently to create sustainability within your team. Lastly, I host a team meeting to recognize accomplishments within my team and set the mood for the new month. People love to be recognized for their hard work and accomplishments. This also creates a stronger bond with your team and helps them see they're a part of something much bigger.

These are just a few examples of what I personally do to ensure my business grows daily. It may look different for you in your business, but it should give you a better idea of how you can better organize your time in the future. Here's a more specific breakdown of the tasks you should be focusing your energy on as a Network Marketer.

All Income Producing Activities

- Add to your prospecting list (who do you want to connect with? Who do you want to build a stronger bond with? Add to this list each day)
- Send invites (to look at your opportunity)
- Present (through live video and in-person on the opportunity)

- Follow-up (past customers and hosts)
- Close (make the sale, book events, signup new teammates)
- Team build (check-in with your team, team calls, meetings, and trainings)
- Post on Social Media (curiosity posts, invites to upcoming events, use a call to action)

Think about your onboarding process for new team members. Are they spending their time doing the right tasks starting out? Is everything you teach them, necessary? Your onboarding program is your first impression, so keep it simple. If you overwhelm new members, they're less likely to stick around. Remember the acronym K.I.S.S or "Keep It Simple, Sweetheart." Keep things as simple as possible, while still delivering the important information they need starting out. Teach them about these income producing activities. Their business should fit within their lifestyle. When in doubt, go back and remember: Book, Sell, Recruit. Rinse and Repeat.

Dracy: IPA's, DIBB, DIMM & ROI's

- **IPA's:** Income Producing Activities
- **DIBB:** Does It Build Your Business?
- **DIMM:** Does It Make Me Money?
- **ROI's:** Return on Investment

The keyword is *productivity*: be productive, not busy.

What are your IPA's? Do they build your business and make you money? Do you get a return on investment? The investment we are talking about, is the investment of time and you.

Time Management is a key skill you can continually improve on and invest time in. The best course I ever took in my first year of business was a time management course. This set the foundation to my continued success. The first year, I did everything with raw enthusiasm, but eventually burnt out. Review and reflect on where you put your energy. What is going to be the best use of your time?

When you BYOB or "Be Your Own Boss," you get to own your time. Run your own schedule. Most people start with this being a side hustle and have limited time to invest. Use your time wisely— know your company's IPA's or Income Producing Activities.

In this industry, systems are in place for onboarding and leadership development. The Activities are very well laid out so you do not have to figure them out. Meet people. Identify their needs and give them what they want. Make appointments, hold presentations either on or offline. The goal is to give a customer experience. Discover their needs and show them how you can deliver products they love that make their life more enjoyable, flexible, gives them more freedom, money, and an opportunity to have a bright future.

Activities That Build Your Business (DIBB's)

Educate: Educate people on the products and business. How much time and what you focus on will be your future rewards. This is where you work out how much time on selling your products, and how much time on promoting your business, recruiting and leadership development. Your rewards will come from sharing the benefits of all these categories. Educate in a way that gives them short, step by step ways to improve the quality of their lives, whether it be by the products or opportunity.

Empower: You become empowering by sharing your story, sharing your growth, overcoming challenges, learning and what you are doing to be of service to others.

These are key elements to be aware of its importance to selling your position. Your progress will make you and your business attractive.

Your progress will make you and your business attractive.

Activities That Make You Money (DIMM's)

Engage: Prospecting and lead generation. How do you engage online and offline? Decide how much time you'll invest daily in your everyday networking activities. Meet people and pay attention. Listening and communication skills are important. Master your approach.

Exposure: Get in front of people, online and in-person presentations. Educate and empower.

Enroll: Get the YES, the sale, the new recruit. To become great at enrolling, become great at practicing the offer and closing, daily. Use the same script over and over. Upsell, overcome objections, and help them solve their problems. Take them on a journey. Work through their needs and give them what they want.

How to Prioritize Your Activities

Step 1. Write down the required activities and responsibilities to build your business.

Step 2. Identify your DIBB and DIMM activities. Find a balance between the two. DIBB's are your planning, content and posts. DIMM's are your events and presentations.

Step 3. Make a schedule. Decide on the time and allocate that on your planner.

What are your daily, weekly, monthly, and quarterly annual activities?

Daily 6 C's

- **Challenge:** Personal development and challenges you set for yourself that day.
- **Care Calls:** Customer and VIP's.
- **Conversations:** Leads. Invite people to showcase your products and opportunity.
- **Content Creation:** Social Media, newsletters, and blogs. Perks, benefits, training, business, product, show and tell.
- **Chats:** Teammates to praise progress, celebrate milestones, discuss challenges and their 6 C's for the day.
- **Coaching Call:** New teammates, Future Leaders.

Schedule Weekly Events & Presentations (Online & Offline)

Be consistent and make it happen.

Minimum Once per Week

- Event to showcase your products
- Event to showcase your opportunity 1 on 1 or 1 to many
- Personal Coaching call with your Upline

Monthly

- Team Meeting
- Onboarding Training
- Future Leader Training
- Leader Training

Quarterly

- Team Celebration and Collaboration

Annually

- Convention
- Incentive Trip

I love to work this out. I have a date with myself every quarter to work out my schedule with a highlighter — I highlight my personal business, events, training, and personal time. This sells my position when people see my calendar.

I love operating on a week-at-a-glance and month-at-a-glance. After 30 years, I review my daily plan like it is the most important part of my day. The days I don't do reviews are those days I'm busy but not productive.

Your best ROI's are *you* — invest in yourself to have a Ph.D in Social Skills. Learn, study, read books & material around the following topics: Love Languages, Personality Types, Time Management, Communication Skills, Making an Impact, First Impressions, and Leadership.

> *"Investing in yourself is the best investment you will ever make. It will improve your life and the lives of those around you."*
> — *Robin Sharma*

Chapter 9: The Gift of Selling Your Position

Teisha: Sell Yourself!

"Selling is not something you do to someone.
It's something you do for someone."
— Zig Ziglar

Selling yourself is easier said than done. If there is one thing that people have a hard time doing, it's sharing accomplishments. You may feel like you're bragging about yourself, or feel worried about what others think.

However, there are many ways to sell your position and be humble at the same time. If you're worried about coming across as over-confident or arrogant, know that you will *never* be portrayed this way. If your heart is in the right place, it will come across and be heard that way to others.

This topic has me reflecting back on all the interviews I've had for the variety of jobs I've pursued. "Confidence" did not describe me in an interview scenario. I remember my mom telling me, "Teisha, you need to sell yourself." Deep down, she knew this was not my strong suit. I hated talking about myself. I disliked being the center of attention in a conversation. I felt awkward and not qualified for what I was doing.

I've always been a life-long learner. I love to learn new things. If I had an interview coming up, I researched beforehand to learn everything about that job. However, I would get caught up in the part where I needed to be perfect. I felt like I needed to say things that I didn't agree with to land the job. I felt as if I needed to memorize what I was going to say so that it was something that they wanted to hear. Interviews were at the top of my fear list with public speaking. I've landed every job I've interviewed for, but I was not myself. It's something that I'm disappointed in today. Unfortunately, that's how it is in some industries.

You may be wondering why I am a leader today. This is another reason I chose to pursue entrepreneurship. I get to be the one in charge of my own business and be the interviewer of the people I want to work with. But that still doesn't explain how I got into leadership. If I wasn't confident in what I was doing and couldn't share my accomplishments with others, why would anyone want to be part of my team? It's simple: when you find what you are unbelievably passionate about, all you have to do is be yourself and you will attract others from miles away.

Actions Speak Louder Than Words

You already know my "accidental leader" story. I had no intention of becoming a leader and impacting others through this business opportunity. But because of my burning passion and contagious excitement, people naturally were drawn to me. I didn't have to brag about myself or tell others why they should be a part of *my* team. Actions speak louder than words. People are emotional beings. When people see the vulnerability and emotions that I portray when it comes to what I do, *that* sells it to them.

My mentor Dracy told me, "You have to be bad before you're good, and good before you're great."

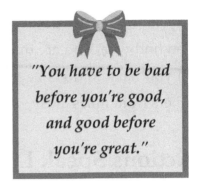

"You have to be bad before you're good, and good before you're great."

I didn't display most of these qualities before starting my Network Marketing business. These skills were learned through courage to try, patience through setbacks, and consistency with everything I did.

What made the biggest difference in my business? My mindset. I had a *huge* shift in mindset over the last few years. Your mindset must be strong, with no cracks. As soon as there are cracks, your confidence in what you do suffers, and so does your prospects' belief in you.

Never Stop Sharing Your "Why"

Selling your position is not something you're doing to someone, it's something that you're doing for someone. If you joined a Network Marketing company, something drew you to it. If you were

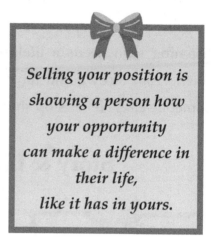

Selling your position is showing a person how your opportunity can make a difference in their life, like it has in yours.

drawn to it, that means millions of others will be drawn by the same things that you were.

Selling your position is showing a person how your opportunity can make a difference in their life, like it has in yours.

Do this by sharing your story. Sometimes, that includes sharing your accomplishments, because you need to. For instance, if I hadn't shared what type of person I was before I got into this industry, people would never know the transformation I went through. I would never relate to people.

Nobody is perfect— when you portray that "perfect lifestyle," it's hard for people to see themselves in your position. People relate to real-life struggles, small wins and the little things. Everyone needs to hear your story because even if it speaks to only one person out there listening who needs a lifeline, you may be that for them. Your story could have an immense impact on someone else. Never stop sharing your "why."

Story & Lifestyle

Stop selling features and benefits. Start selling the story and the lifestyle.

You could "sell" your products all day long, but when you start sharing the stories behind the products and how it's impacted you and others, that's when you'll make the sale. When it comes to your opportunity, it's the same thing. Stop selling features and benefits. Start selling the story and the lifestyle. If you're in this for the long haul, you need to remember that you're selling a lifestyle, not a product.

Selling your position is not just about you. It should be about the prospect. Your role is to ask questions and to be a good listener. Share pieces of your story when it's relevant.

For example, if someone inquires about doing what you do, know that they are going to have a different path to success than you. They have different skills and abilities. Identify those— help them understand why and how those specific skills will help them succeed.

You are the interviewer. The more information you have, the easier it is to sell your position. Find out what initially piqued their interest. What are they looking to get out of this? A Network Marketing business does a whole lot more than give someone extra income. Uncover their "why" and be a good listener.

Once you know, tell them exactly what will be required of them to achieve the goals they want to achieve. Don't sugar coat it. There is nothing worse than false expectations. Be upfront and real so they gain trust in you. Share why their specific skills and abilities will help them succeed in reaching their goals. If you show confidence that they will succeed, they will have that belief in themselves too.

What to Say

I've always struggled with "what to say" when people ask what I do for a living. If you're a full-time Network Marketer like me, it can be difficult to explain this role to an unfamiliar person. The goal of the answer is not to provide a fancy title, but create curiosity and get people wanting to hear more. Here are some responses I've used that may help you feel more confident in "what you do" when asked:

Example 1: I'm an entrepreneur. "I help others with _____ by doing _____." This example is open ended. Fill in the blanks with who you help and how you help them.

Example 2: I'm a Network Marketer. "I help others start their own business that fits into their lifestyle so they can create residual income for themselves and their families." This example is for Network Marketers looking to build their teams and make an impact on others.

Example 3: I'm in the health and wellness industry. "I help people who struggle with _____ by offering ____." This example gets specific to your product or service. Identify the type of industry you're in, insert a problem your target market has, and your solution to that problem.

"Selling your position" is about genuinely showing confidence in what you do, so you can share your passion naturally with others. It's not about

The best product you have to sell is your position.

memorizing what you think people want to hear, but sharing the story of where you started and how far you have come. People want to know the real you and believe they can trust you to guide them.

The best product you have to sell is your position.

Dracy: Your #1 Goal and Role Is To Sell Your Position

Three Positions You Sell

1. Showcase your business to customers so they want to do what you do— become a distributor/consultant

2. Showcase leadership to your distributor or consultant so they want to become a leader

3. Showcase the highest ranks so your leaders want to help people become leaders and have a legacy income

Everything you do and say is Selling Your Position. How you shine, how you handle difficult situations, and how you help people get what they want. How you have fun, how we love and share the love.

You are always being watched. People watch and pay attention to see if they can do what you do. Do they want to invest their number one commodity (time) in you? Are you worth spending their time learning about this business?

They want to see if you show up daily with good intentions, and if you can show them the way. Have a Mission, Vision and Passion. Get your MVP on.

Have a Mission, Vision and Passion. Get your MVP on.

Mission, Vision & Passion

MISSION: What is your calling? Why are you doing what you are doing? Who are you helping and what difference are you making? This is your core purpose and your present cause. What is the reason for your goals? Define this with a road map, strategy and action plan that comes from the heart and people will want to hear you roar.

VISION: What is that clear mental image of your future? Where are you going? How will you get there? Who will you bring with you? What are your long-term aspirations and goals? Describe it, create a picture-perfect story where your audience sees themselves as one of the cast members.

PASSION: This is the energy you bring to the table that makes you attractive.

Sell Your Position

1. Think of a window storefront. How does a merchant designer set up a storefront so it entices you to walk in that store?

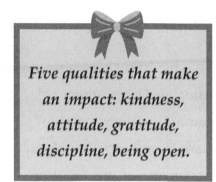

Five qualities that make an impact: kindness, attitude, gratitude, discipline, being open.

First Impressions — are you trustworthy, competent, likable, confident? Do you have status or authority? Are you approachable?

Five qualities that make an impact: kindness, attitude, gratitude, discipline, being open.

2. Eye candy. What makes the business look sweet, so someone would want a taste?

The benefits of network marketing are: flexibility and time freedom, self development, travel, free business training, free mentorship, leverage, low financial risk, tax benefits, work from anywhere around the world, and residual income.

3. How do you demonstrate the lifestyle potential? What trips have you been able to take, such as family holidays? Talk about time off.

What have you been able to purchase to make your life easier or more enjoyable? What experiences and memories have you made? Get good at planting seeds. Share subliminally about all that you do, in conversations, presentations and posts.

4. If you were a commercial, what would you want them to know about your offer? What has been your personal transformation from the products and business?

What difference are you making in the lives of others?

The power of testimonies is your best commercial. Have raving fans talk about how you helped them.

5. If you had a "Hiring" sign out your storefront, what would you be looking for in an applicant? This is your opportunity to get what you want by putting it out there.

Write on a piece of paper what qualities and the type of person you would like to have on your team. Share it. What you talk about, comes about.

Create content that asks, "Are you open to learning new things?" "Do you like adventure and owning your own time?" Look for someone that is fun, has a positive attitude, and likes helping people.

Ask people who you know that are outgoing, or the most enthusiastic person they know. Tell people what you are looking for. *Believe* you have something amazing to share. Live it and share it daily. If you believe, people will believe in *you*.

What Not To Do

- Talk about other people behind their backs
- Be negative about a person or situation
- Look stressed or say "I'm so busy"
- Unorganized or late
- Blame others for anything
- Not make time for people
- Not coachable
- Don't attend the company events
- Try to be like someone else

Make people feel special. Mary Kay shared in her book, "You Can Have It All" that she imagined people had sticky notes on their foreheads saying "make me feel special." Your one role in this business is to make people feel special, worthy, and a part of something.

Six Principles That Will Help You Get The Most Out of Selling Your Position

1. You are not the center of the universe — other people are.

2. Pay attention to other peoples' lives. This is the secret to connection.

3. In conversation, it is far better to be interested than interesting.

4. Consciously move the emphasis from "what's in it for you?" to "what's in it for them?"

5. The more you contribute to the lives of others, the more will be given to you.

6. In every meaningful interaction, resolve that the other person will leave feeling better about themselves than when they arrived.

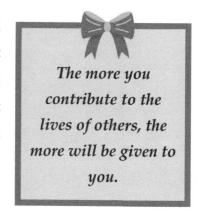

The more you contribute to the lives of others, the more will be given to you.

Objective to Events and Company Functions

- Build relationships
- Include people
- Create identity
- Personally welcome
- Recognition
- Edification
- Get feedback
- Always have a call to action
- Gifting
- Follow up
- Most important: *fun!*

This is you leading by example and creating masters in the Art of Selling your Position.

This is Recruiting 101.

Chapter 10: The Gift of Consistency

Teisha: Your Success Lies In Your Routine

"If you are persistent, you will get it.
If you are consistent, you will keep it."
—*Harvey Mackay*

Consistency sets the successful and the unsuccessful apart in this industry. Most people do not have what it takes to stay consistent, but you do. I know you do because you're reading this book. Most people have a hard time being consistent because they want to see immediate results. You and I know that this is not a "get rich quick" scheme.

It's the same idea with weight loss. Many people want to lose weight, but when they find out what's required, they opt out. People can be persistent and commit until they see results. However, once they see the results, many think they've hit their goal and stop.

This is where consistency comes in. Like weight loss, network marketing is a lifestyle change. Keep going. Overcome obstacles and be self-motivated. No matter what difficult situations come into your personal life or your business, keep going.

However, you are still a human being. Shit happens and you need breaks. I get it— just don't let that "break" lead to quitting your dream. Your leader may not tell you this, but I will, because you need to hear it. If you look for excuses to take breaks, or you utilize any life hiccup as an excuse to stop working on your business, you will never make it.

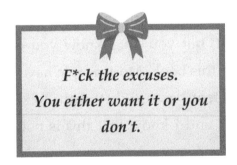

**F*ck the excuses.
You either want it or you
don't.**

F*ck the excuses. You either want it or you don't.

I seriously get it. Life happens, but your "why" should be strong enough to get you through *anything*. Your goals may need to be pushed back a little bit further, but *do not quit*.

Treat Your Business Like A Business

Don't be a "Roller Coaster Network Marketer"— the person who shows up one month and ghosts their business the next. It is not sustainable. How can you expect people to show up for you in your business if you don't show up for them? Building trust with people requires consistency. Touch your business every day to make it big.

Treat your business like a business and not like a hobby. This is the first step to achieving consistency. If you have a regular 9-5 job now, you

Treat your business like a business and not like a hobby.

have a responsibility to show up on time, do your work properly, and perform daily tasks. Similarly, you must develop a routine in this industry. Your success lies in having a routine.

Every typical 9-5 job has a routine. You wake up in the morning, get ready for work and do your job. You have tea or coffee breaks, and a lunch break. In between, you focus on your work because you must accomplish so much in a day before going home.

When you work from home, it's trickier. There are more distractions, and you are required to hold yourself accountable. Working from home is challenging because you must be consistent with the "mental side." Thoughts run through your mind about ending the day early or taking an extra hour for lunch, but if you don't put the work into your business, the business will not work for you. Treat your business like a business, not like a hobby. Hobbies don't make you money, but businesses do.

You may have chosen the path of Network Marketing to create your own hours, oversee yourself, and have the opportunity to make an uncapped income. Who wouldn't want that? But that doesn't mean you can slack off. It's called Net-"Work" Marketing for a reason. The beginning requires extra effort to create your pages, build your brand, and create systems for your team to follow and duplicate what you've created.

I *love* automating systems in my business to make my life easier. However, you cannot be replaced by automated robots— they will not lead a successful team. Consistently show up for your customers and your team.

Intentional Consistency: Set Yourself Up for Success

I can't express enough how important consistency is in your business. It's literally everything! If you don't have consistency, you have nothing. This is a relationship building business. You build and strengthen relationships with others through consistent connection. If you stop showing up, you stop building relationships. When you stop building relationships, you don't have a successful Network Marketing business. It's EASY math! 1+1=2.

Here are my top four tips for having more consistency in your business and being more intentional about it:

1. Remember WHY You Are Here. Your "why" is the purpose that fuels your passion in your business.

If your "why" is important to you, then so should your consistency be in your business. You will have your good and bad days. You will have steady and slow months. But the one thing that will always remain consistent in your business is your WHY.

Figure out why you started this journey. What has this business helped you with since getting started? Is that important to you? What fuels you in your business?

Whether your "why" is to put food on the table for your family, put your kids through school sports, give yourself some well-deserved time, to help pay the bills, or because it makes you happy and reduces your mental stress, *is it important!*

My vision board is on my office wall where I sit. Anytime I'm struggling in my business, forgetting what I should be doing, or experiencing that cloudiness in my head, I reflect on my vision board. It's about my "why" and reminds me to keep going.

2. Don't Set The Bar Too High For Yourself. I encourage you to *dream big*, while also setting SMART goals: Specific, Measurable, Achievable, Relevant, Timely.

I used to struggle with having too high an expectation for myself. I struggled with this every time I would decide that I was going to "be healthy." I would try and implement all of these things in one day and it was *never* sustainable for me. I was a rollercoaster when it came to goal-setting.

For instance, I would try to eat super healthy, restrict myself from my favorite things, work out every single day, and almost starve myself for some meals, trying to use portion control. I realized how unhealthy and unsustainable that was, because it only lasted days.

When you restrict yourself from the things you love and are used to doing every day, change is unbelievably difficult. It is the same with Network Marketing. If you're new and have never ever made a sale, booked an event, or brought in a new team member, you have a lot to learn. You can't do it all at once. Start with the basics and do one thing at a time. In fact, good things do take time. When your to-do list is *full* and you're trying to get it done in a record amount of time, you won't know where to begin.

Start small and give yourself bite-sized, manageable tasks. Start with a goal that is achievable but slightly uncomfortable. Get comfortable with being uncomfortable in your business. Then, absolutely destroy that goal and cheer for your damn self! After you've consistently met that goal, the following month you can set that goal even higher and just rinse and repeat the same steps you did to accomplish the goal the first time. Failure is a part of success. You only fail if you don't take it as a learning lesson and keep going.

3. Put It On The Calendar. Let's be real: if it's not on the calendar, it ain't gonna happen!

If you know you need to do follow-ups a month from now, put it in your calendar now. If you need to follow up with a few people regarding bookings the following week, write it down. I personally use two calendars to set myself up for success and stay consistent. I use a large monthly desk calendar so that I can see my entire month in front of me. I also have my weekly calendar that helps me stay organized and know my goals for that week only. I review my week every Sunday and make sure I have everything from my monthly calendar written onto my upcoming weekly calendar. I don't care how simple the task is, write it down. Mix your personal life and business tasks on these calendars to ensure you get the Income Producing Activities (IPA's) done without interruptions.

For instance, if that means you need to schedule when you will do the laundry, pick up the kids, go to your appointment, have date night with your partner, go grocery shopping, or meal prep... do just that.

When looking over my monthly calendar, I fill it in with my non-negotiables and personal life tasks first, because family always comes first. Next, enter your business tasks, training, and team calls. Consistently follow that calendar. Highlight those tasks on your weekly calendar after you've completed them. I make sure that I do not flip that page for next week until *all* my tasks are highlighted. If you don't put it on the calendar, you're not going to do it. Plain and simple.

4. Work With The End In Mind. What do you want to get out of your goals that you set for yourself?

Now that you know your end goal, break down the action steps to get there. Let's say your big goal is to make a 6-figure income. That's an amazing goal, but what does it really look like to get there?

You won't do this in a few days. What must you do to make 6 figures? For you, that might look like "X" amount in personal sales per month. Perhaps it means bringing in "X" amount of new team members monthly and hosting "X" amount of events each month.

In order to do "X" amount of sales, how many events is that? When you have that number, figure out how many people you must talk to about hosting. How many people do you need to talk to about the business opportunity this month?

Break it down into manageable, bite-sized tasks to reach that big goal. Consider your vision and what you need to do each month to get one step closer to your goal. Then, dig deeper and break up those monthly tasks into weekly tasks so that you continue to touch your business each day.

Break it down into manageable, bite-sized tasks to reach that big goal.

Dracy: Show Up No Matter What

Consistency connects the dots. Consistency is key. You can do everything else outstanding, but if you are not consistent, you will not succeed.

Consistently show up no matter what, if you want to achieve real success. Consistency is a reflection of your behavior, your habits and your character.

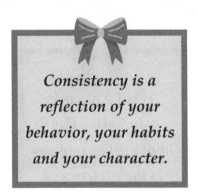

Consistency is a reflection of your behavior, your habits and your character.

What should you be consistent in?

- **Values:** What is important?
- **Principles:** Your standards and beliefs
- **Action:** Do what is important daily with passion
- Passion + Consistency = **Success.**

Consistency is more important than perfection. There is no sense aiming for perfection if you want to make money.

My motto is "speed before perfection". Have a set of core values, know your standards, and know what you need to do daily (IPA's) with continual improvements, to turn your passion into real success.

This process keeps it simple and duplicatable. Bring consistent duplication into the mix to reap the rewards of multiplication. That is Network Marketing.

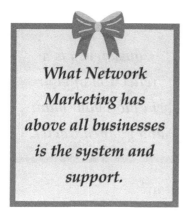

What Network Marketing has above all businesses is the system and support.

This business is not easy, and no business of any sort is easy. What Network Marketing has above all businesses is the system and support. It's simple if you stick to the system that is provided to you. Get to work on yourself first, and the systems will get easier.

I recently went kayaking. I couldn't help reflecting on my life experiences. I paddled with the wind at my back. I was going with the tide.

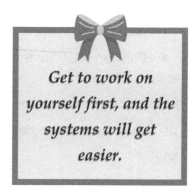

Get to work on yourself first, and the systems will get easier.

Super easy, fun and absolutely spectacular, but when the tides changed and I was going against the wind, it became a much different experience— still kayaking but a different experience.

I had to put on a mental game. I had to focus on my end result, break the journey up in small milestones, keep my head down and consistently paddle. Every time I slowed down or stopped, I was taken so far back that it didn't feel like I was going anywhere.

The only way I was going to make it to my destination was to consistently paddle, take small breaks at my milestones, and keep going. In the end, I made it, and it was rewarding knowing the effort needed when it became challenging, but with the right push and focus on consistency, I made it to my destination.

6 Steps to Being OUTRAGEOUSLY Consistent

1. Start with a Consistent Morning. Morning routine has been proven to set your mind up in a state of controlled focus.

How you spend the morning sets you up for the rest of your day. It increases your productivity and you will feel more in control of your day's activities. Develop a consistent morning habit to help with your habits,

191

lower your stress, and give yourself enough time for important things.

2. Write it down: F.O.C.U.S. Follow One Course Until Success. It's easier to be consistent when your behavior isn't erratic and distracted.

Write it down and focus on completing it, one to do at a time. Do the hard things first.

3. Consistent Thinking. To have consistent behavior, strive for consistent thinking.

Read the right material. Program your brain on the things you want to do, be and have. This helps in your efforts to stay focused. Review and rehearse your daily outcomes and accomplishments.

4. Don't let self-doubt creep in. Doubt kills more dreams than failure ever will.

The shadows in your mind try to manipulate your thoughts, but this can't happen when you follow the other steps to consistency. Create positive affirmations and read them daily, especially if your shadows linger longer than they should.

5. Just do it, even if you don't feel like it. Sometimes, you don't feel like pursuing some tasks.

You will find yourself grateful and happy that you pushed through the momentary discomfort. This helps define your character and the tasks become easier. However, if it continues to give you no joy and uncertainty, maybe you need to revisit the task, the goal, or your purpose.

6. Improve your consistency by consistently improving. Don't let the definition of insanity of "doing the same thing over and over and expecting different results" get in the way. Instead, do the same thing over and over again, while improving upon it. The beauty about consistency is that it permits you to be incremental in your progress.

"Be faithful in small things
because it is in them that your strength lies."
—*Mother Teresa*

Chapter 11: The Gift of Social Media

Teisha: I Want to See You Win

Running my business through Social Media is my favorite thing to do and teach. Besides being a full-time Network Marketer, I also casually do Social Media Management for other companies on the side. It helps me strengthen my own knowledge on social platforms and gives me the opportunity to help others grow their brand, another huge passion of mine.

I want to see *everyone* win! I'm unbelievably passionate about Social Media and helping others grow online, while building strong connections with others. I've been growing my business online since the beginning. When Network Marketing first became popular, it was all about the in-home events and face-to-face interaction. Now, social media is taking over the Network Marketing industry. People want to navigate how to run their business online.

Being a Millennial and on the verge of a Gen Z, I've had all the Social Media platforms and enjoyed using their features. When I started in Network Marketing, I took a leading role in running a professional business online. I made all the mistakes starting out. I've learned from them and continue to be innovative in my business. I love to teach others how to be successful online as well.

Social media can be a monumental fear to many people when it comes to running an online business, especially the Generation X and the Boomers. The reason for this is because there are so many social media platforms out there now and it can be overwhelming to try and do it all.

Social Media Used to Be So Simple

It keeps getting more complex. For instance, Facebook used to be a way to network with close friends and family. People made statuses to talk about what they were doing every day. Today, you rarely see people making statuses. They've added a marketplace for selling used items. You no longer need to have a garage sale because you can post everything online.

You can create events and groups to network with others on common interests. You can create stories, do live videos, and make reels for entertainment. There is *so much new* technology! If you don't stay up to date with new features, it's easy to get lost and feel overwhelmed.

Instagram, now owned by Facebook, used to be a platform for sharing photos. Today, we can share pictures, videos, create stories, create reels, go live, send personal messages, create guides, and shop. We can also search hashtags and locations to network with people.

It's no longer simple. However, it is innovative and can be a *huge* benefit to running your Network Marketing business online. There are other platforms such as TikTok, LinkedIn, WhatsApp, Snapchat, Pinterest, Twitter, and the list goes on. Did I overwhelm you yet? I promise, it wasn't my intention. My intention was to sympathize with you because I get it. It's a learning curve for many.

Where do you start? Master one or two platforms. Just like setting SMART goals, do not try to do it all.

It's better to be a master in a few things than mediocre in everything.

My personal favorite platforms that are the best for a Network Marketing business are Facebook and Instagram. However, you need to create your own brand because social media is not always reliable. These are *free* platforms. If Facebook and Instagram randomly shut down tomorrow, would you still have a business? If the answer is no, then think outside the box. Collect emails and save a list of your customers. Have a Plan B.

Instagram

This platform has many different features you can use to help grow your business. They make it easy to find and network with your target audience. Who do you serve? What do those people search for?

For example, if your product promotes weight loss, search Instagram for other weight loss accounts. Every person who is following that account is probably your target audience.

Consider hashtags that your target audience may be using on their posts: #WeightLoss #LoseWeight #HealthyChoices #HealthIsWealth. These are just a few examples of hashtags that people may be using. When you search those hashtags, you can connect with people who have common interests.

Connect with people in your area by searching locations. Search your city's location on Instagram and look through posts. Show love through liking people's posts, leave genuine comments, and follow people you think you would click with.

On the flip side, use hashtags and locations in your posts, so people can find you. Many people have reached out to me and said, "I found your Instagram account through this hashtag." Those messages led to new sales, new hosts, and even new team members. You never know where a new connection will take you. In my opinion, Instagram is *the best* platform for networking and meeting new people.

Stories & Reels

Another feature on Instagram that helps strengthen your connections with your current followers is stories. Through stories, people get to know the real you. Show up authentically every day and let people know what you've been up to. Within stories, there are engagement features such as: polls, quizzes, questions, links, and more. I utilize one or more of these every day. They are fun, engaging, and people love them.

A new "Quick Growth Feature" you *need* to jump on ASAP on Instagram is Reels. If you know what a TikTok video is, it's like that but on Instagram. Reels are short and crisp videos that grab your audience's attention.

If you're anything like me, you could scroll through reels for hours. They're addictive and entertaining. Use reels to educate about who you help and how you help them, in fun ways. I don't care how old you are. *You can do reels.* You do not need to jump and dance to do them. Like any new feature Instagram releases, jump on them right away because the platform will reward you for trying out new features. Rewards come through views and exposure.

Views explode on reels. I recently had a reel reach over 200,000 views. I gained a ton of exposure and followers. The reel didn't have much to do with my business, but so many people related to me and wanted to follow me for more content. These new followers are exposed to my other brand pillars that I talk about on my platform.

Brand Pillars

Speaking of brand pillars, let's talk about those and why you need them. Constantly coming up with content can be a daunting task. How do successful business owners do it every single day? The best strategy is to identify your brand pillars (three to five) and create content around each pillar every week.

Discover your brand pillars by writing down *everything* that brings you joy. Once you have a list of 30+ words, group similar ideas to create one pillar. At least one of your pillars should be in line with your industry. Pillar examples include: Mom Life, Farm Living, Mental Health Advocate, Health and Wellness, Confidence, Leadership, Sports, or Baking.

Once you have pillars, write down your story for each one. When you share content, choose a small piece of your story for a specific pillar to share that day. Now you have never-ending content for your social media.

Instagram is an excellent platform for networking, meeting new people, and converting them into leads.

Facebook

This platform is excellent for creating that sense of community in your business and strengthening current relationships that you already have. My goal is to drive people from Instagram into my Facebook community.

Your online community is where all the magic happens. When referring to "community", I'm talking about your private customer group. Although my favorite platform is Instagram, I use Facebook most for running my business. Unlike Instagram, you can create groups on Facebook, which help us as Network Marketers build community with customers and run online events.

However, your profile is not as discoverable as it would be on Instagram. People don't search for hashtags and locations as much as they do on Instagram. The focus of Facebook should be to strengthen bonds with your current friends list and customers. Refer back to the community chapter for more tips on building community within your private customer groups on Facebook.

Connect List

To build stronger connections with people on your friends list, create a "Connect List." This is a list of people you want to be more intentional about connecting with. Go through your friends list — that list probably started a long time ago. Write down the names of people you haven't connected with in a while — perhaps an old friend from high school or college, or an acquaintance you met this one time at that one place. Whatever the reason they're on your friends list, jot them down on your connect list.

If you're not connecting with others, Facebook isn't showing any of their content to you, and vice versa. When you connect with someone by liking their post, commenting, replying to their story, or private messaging, Facebook knows you are friends and will show your content to each other. This strengthens the relationships with people already on your list.

Every day, set time aside to network. Look at your connect list and choose five people on that list to connect with, in some way. When you show interest in their content by liking, leaving a genuine comment, or replying to their story, they will notice your name and start to check out your content. The Facebook algorithm will be in your favor and show more people your content.

Facebook Parties: Events & Groups

Another way we use Facebook is through the events and groups feature to throw online events or parties. Your online events should follow these four E's: Engaging, Educational, Entertaining and Empowering.

- **Engaging** posts invite customers to comment and give their opinions. This could look like a "Roll Call" post, a "This or That" post, or a fun party game to break the ice.
- **Educational** posts teach your customers about products, people, and programs.
- **Entertaining** posts could be live videos where you demo a product or service you offer.
- **Empowering** posts get people excited about something. They capture people's attention and leave them curious to find out more. You may empower others through speaking about your WHY in your business, or perhaps what this opportunity has done for you and your family.

When you hit the four E's in your Facebook events, you're bound to grow your business online.

5 Things To Stop Doing On Social Media

Now that we've talked about what you SHOULD be doing on social media and how to do those things, let's quickly touch on what NOT to do.

1. Don't be a walking billboard for your company. If people want to see all the stock photos from your company's profile, they will follow them.

2. Don't be someone that you're not. Genuinely be yourself to succeed. Don't be and say what you think others want to hear. Just be you.

3. Don't spam people. Don't send a million copy/paste messages to people asking them to buy your product. They never asked for that info and the answer is always going to be no. Take the time to build the relationships.

4. Never compare your online business to others. Everyone starts at a different spot in their business. If other people's accounts have you comparing it to your own, unfollow them and focus on growing *you*.

5. Stop trying to give ALL the information. Word vomit is a real thing. Less is more. The less information you can give on posts and in videos, the more interested and curious people become.

Social Media can be intimidating, but my university professor told me, "If you want to learn how to do something, just jump in and do it." He was 100% right. That's

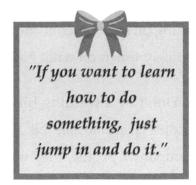

"If you want to learn how to do something, just jump in and do it."

how I went from shy to outgoing and from fearful to confident. You'll never succeed if you don't try. If you need a little extra motivation, go back to the consistency chapter and that should give you a kick in the butt.

Dracy: The Non-Negotiables

"Your smile is your logo,
your personality is your business card,
how you make people feel after having an experience
with you becomes your trademark."
— *Jay Danzie*

As much as business has changed over the years and how fast it is changing daily, these are three things you do not want to change. Unless, of course, you do not smile, your personality sucks, and you don't give people warm fuzzies. In that case, if you are not willing to work on these three non-negotiables you are definitely in the wrong business. Because you are reading this, I do not believe this is you.

I may have been in business for almost 30 years but every day I am learning new things.

Social media is the way of doing business, no matter who you are, or what generation you come from. It's part of the process of working on *you*. If you don't work out how it can work for you, you may as well call yourself an expert in being a Social Butterfly rather than a Social Media Magnet. On average, the lifespan of an adult butterfly is 2 to 3 weeks. Like a butterfly, you might be pretty today, but you could be gone tomorrow. Planning out your social media is an important piece of your overall business strategy.

I am no expert on this topic. I am currently a student and this is what I am learning. *Content-content-content* and *give-value-give-value-give-value*. Something you can do — you only work out "how" and "where." If you want engagement, you must give engagement.

This is your opportunity and space to show up, be present and let people see you unwrap your gifts. Let them see you go from the caterpillar to the butterfly they will remember, talk about, and share. Let that be the goal: create such great content, people will share it.

Branding You

I am passionate about Personal Branding. *You.* Since my favorite topic is "you", personal branding is exciting for me. Network Marketing used to be about the company first and you second.

People are more likely to connect with you and your values. Your customers can be with you for a lifetime through your journeys, passions, recommendations, challenges, and triumphs. Attach yourself to a company that has a successful track record of not just great products, but great people and great programs that make a difference.

Connect with your customers through your social media platforms (Instagram, Facebook, and groups). The biggest gift you can give your audience is to allow them to watch you unwrap your inner leader, so they can celebrate your success journey with you. Many of your people will go from customer, to distributor, to leaders, and repeat the process.

Your job is to share and show people why and the way. Back in the day, you traveled from one-on-one meetings in the coffee shop, presentation to presentation in the living room, meeting to meeting in the hotel, driving from town to town, flying from city to city, just to get in front of the people and present your product and company presentation.

Now that social media exists, your audience is in the millions. It's not just the company's presentation you are sharing; it's your transformation, and you get to do it daily in front of the masses.

Be brave, vulnerable, and just do it. You get to earn while you learn. That hasn't changed. Your personal development has not changed. What has changed is that you can decide to do it a lot faster than ever before without having to leave your home. You also have the opportunity to work from anywhere versus working from home.

The same skills and personal development are still there. The difference is you get to share the behind the scenes, the good, the bad and the ugly. This is what people want to see.

This is hard for us seasoned players coming from an era of "fake it till you make it." No social media or multiple platforms, just good old fashion phones attached to the wall, no videos. Wow, that does show my age.

My business exploded when mobile phones came in the picture, then the internet. This younger generation is already tech savvy, on every platform, and only need to learn about the business work ethic, product benefits and personal development. Fire away.

I am loving the true authenticity and real growth I am getting to see in this younger generation. Gen Z is ambitious, entrepreneurial, tech savvy, with a social conscience. They are just getting started and are going to blow up this industry. We have laid the foundation and they are going to build the towers.

We are all learning together. My "hot shot" Teisha continues to show me the way. Every week, we meet and learn from each other. We are equals. Everyone has something to share and we can learn from everyone. That is what leadership is about.

Teisha came into this industry to master the skills of Network Marketing and social media. She is brave, generous, passionate and hard working. Every day, she shows up to the world and makes it a better place by smiling and sharing her passions. She inspires me. There are many Teisha's out there. You must be open, looking, and having conversations. Find out what people are looking for, and give them what they want. Build that relationship on trust and growth, and you can make this world a better place with loads of opportunities.

Starting with YOU

Image - Intentions – Impact

Know the IMPACT you want to make.
What are your INTENTIONS?
Define your IMAGE.

Image

- Your Story – Your Message
- Style and your packaging are your visuals
- Who you are – What you do
- Vision – Values
- Question to ask yourself – What & Who do you want to attract?
- Focus on the people, not the product. What makes you great is the product. That will shine in the things you do and how you share them to the marketplace.
- Be a product of the product
- Online & Offline
- How are you being perceived?
- Be seen

Intention

- Service above self
- Helping people (emotionally, financially or physically)
- To inspire
- Clear on your values and what you stand for
- Make people happy

Impact

- The difference you are making to your customer, to your community, to the world
- Positive Change
- Healthy Choices
- Healthy Habits
- Transformation
- Overall Beauty

Brand with intentions to serve, not sell. The Pew Research center says 93% of people are influenced online. 65% of your current customers will repurchase or go to the next level with the right influence, support or offer.

Brand with intentions to serve, not sell.

Personal Branding or social media can feel scary and overwhelming, time consuming, and way out of your comfort zone. Here is why it is important to learn...

Five Reasons Personal Branding is Important

1. Inputs Trust
2. Builds Connection
3. Builds Credibility
4. Gains Confidence
5. Gives Authenticity

3 P's to Personal Branding

Purpose - Package – Plan

- Purpose — Mission / Message, Vision / Value
- Package — Image & Visuals
- Plan — Intentions, Impact, Strategy

Your personal brand strategy is no different than how the marketing department for your favorite product develops its communication.

We call it your *style,* and it's your *packaging.*

A brand is not built in a day, a month, or a quarter. It must be strategic and communicated *consistently* over and over before it "works" for you. It's an investment, and as the pieces come into alignment, it creates weight in communicating who you are and why others should trust and invest in *you* and what you offer.

Your 4 V's: Value, Vision , Visuals, Voice = Brand

Be consistent and trust-inspiring. Your "voice" is how you communicate with those you serve and is how you express yourself verbally and non-verbally, so that it is congruent with your vision and values.

If you are on a mission, your vision of who you serve and how you add value must be crystal clear to you and your audience.

Visuals start with your image, appearance, not only in person but how you show up online. I am not talking about old school "dress for success." What you wear has nothing to do with it.

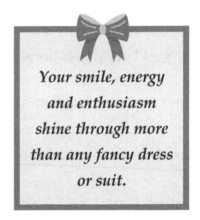

Your smile, energy and enthusiasm shine through more than any fancy dress or suit.

Your smile, energy and enthusiasm shine through more than any fancy dress or suit.

Show up as you are, but make sure you work on your brand and people will see that journey and improvement. *Get help!*

What is Your Objective?

- Grow a tribe
- Share your story
- Educate, truly connect people with solutions
- Create content
- Interaction & engagement

Three Mistakes People Make

1. Incongruent message (saying one thing and doing another)
2. Branding with intentions to sell
3. Branding yourself to be like someone else

Ideas for "Personal" Sharing

- Healthy choices, habits, and quotes
- Choose 8 items that explain you
- Overcoming personal adversity
- Doing what you love
- Things that were hard to do
- Celebrations, milestones, heartfelt moments

Ideas for "Business" Sharing

- Problems and Solutions
- Seeds about your Lifestyle
- Seeds about who you have helped

People look for: Raw, Real, Relevant. Network Marketing is about doing that "One Brave Thing, Every Day." Helping people through social media is just the platform to be all that. Let this be one element that helps you.

People admire your bravery and courage. Do the #onebravething and become an #unwrappedleader.

Next Steps

Leaders are not found, but created. Remember that quote as you continue to develop yourself in this industry and help those on your team.

Writing and working together on this project was the biggest and best self-discovery and development we have ever worked on. Reviewing and reflecting on our life's journey, what we have learned, and want to share, has had so many rewards. We want to encourage you to do the same. This is only just the beginning of your journey and new community to *unwrapping the leader in you.*

These were the topics we felt were most important and wanted to explore with you. What are your personal views, experiences and tips on these topics? What topics would you like to see us explore and share in the future? We want to hear from you!

We even want to challenge you to work with one of your teammates you've coached and write a chapter, or better yet write a book about your story. In fact, we want *you* to become an author in our next book. We want to hear your stories and tips as you get started and develop into a gifted leader. Together, we feel we can unwrap so many gifts together by connecting and sharing in our new platform and community, **The Unwrapped Leader.**

Watch for our "Unwrapped Leader Guide" that will go along with this book to help you unpack these gifts. You can access it on our website, along with free resources to help you step-by-step in unwrapping and exploring your gifts and sharing them with the world.

Sharing your story is the most powerful thing you can do. Your story will inspire, relate to, & empower others to do the same.

Be our next author, shine like a diamond and become an *unwrapped leader*. Visit TheUnwrappedLeader.com for more information on becoming an author in our next book, and staying up to date on upcoming webinars, live online classes, courses and more!

Let's stay connected! Find us on Facebook and Instagram by searching for @TheUnwrappedLeader . We can't wait to watch you begin to share & unpack your story with the world!

Tag us and use our hashtag #TheUnwrappedLeader to be featured.

Remember that
your presence is a gift.

Acknowledgements

Teisha

We need to thank many people for helping make this book possible for each of us. We may be in business *for* ourselves, but we're never *by* ourselves. If it wasn't for the mentors, supporters, doubters, and haters, we would never be as strong as we are today in becoming the unwrapped leaders that we are. It takes an army and we cannot be grateful enough for our team.

I'm forever grateful for my upline, mentor, and friend, **Dracy Dewar**, for introducing me to this incredible industry and continuing to support me, no matter where we both ended up. It just so happens that we started together and ended up together. We knew we couldn't end our stories without each other being a part of it. You've shown me how to develop my gifts in every possible aspect as a Business Builder. I'm thankful for your kindness and wisdom you've given me throughout the years. You have shown me that anything is possible if your passion is strong enough. You are my greatest inspiration.

To my loving partner, **Ryan Zaparniuk**, thank you for always encouraging me to pursue my passions. I'm grateful for the belief you've always had in me to make my dreams come true. You've supported me in so many ways that you'll never know. You stood by me in my decision to follow my heart and take risks. You put my happiness above everything else, and for that, I am forever grateful. I love you so much!

To my mom, **Chantel Ouellette**, thank you for your endless support and showing me what a difference this industry can make. You've always been my biggest cheerleader since day one. Even when you had your doubts or when I told you my next crazy adventure, you were always there to support me and cheer me on for every step of the way. As you like to say, you are essentially my manager. You help me with deliveries, packaging, and anything else I need to serve my customers that aren't within my area. I'm forever thankful for all you've done for me!

To my dad, **Denis Ouellette**, thank you for your support and showing me how to be independent and a hard-worker. You've always been there for me when I needed help with anything. You've taught me how to problem-solve and be of service to others. Thank you for trusting me in my decisions and always being a badass dad.

To my oldest brother, **Dustin Ouellette**, you have paved the path of entrepreneurship in this family. You gave me confidence that I could do this and offered all the support when I chose to get started in this industry. You've never shown an ounce of doubt in my abilities. You've taught me how to be calm and collected in this space. Thank you for your expertise along the way.

To my older brother, **Brandon Ouellette**, you've taught me to never take life too seriously and to live in the moment. You're living proof that a person can never be too old to have fun.

To my mentors, **Melanie Mitro and Katy Ursta**, from Chic Influencer, you've inspired me to chase my North Star. You've taught me how to be a better leader and helped me realize that the best investment you can ever make is in yourself. Thank you for your friendship and support over the last year.

To my team, **The BrewTea Crew**, thank you for believing in me and giving me a chance to lead you. Thank you to those who have been with me from the beginning, and those who have come and gone. You've shown me how the nature of this industry works, and helped me navigate the obstacles that come with leadership. The success stories I've seen come out of this team make me feel proud to do what I do. The impact you've all had on me is tremendous. I love each and every one of you for helping me become the leader and person that I am today.

To my cat, **Earl**, for being my buddy on the days I feel lonely or sad. Working from home is a blessing, but it can be tough as well. You can't read, but I wouldn't be the Cat Mom that I am if I didn't mention you in here. You are simply purr-fect!

To one of my best friends, **Kelsie Davis**, you were the first person who made me feel accepted at my very first leadership summit. You've been there for me through the tough times and great times. Your listening ear is a gift and I can't thank you enough for being my personal therapist and #1 cheerleader (next to my mom) in everything that I do. I fricken love ya from the bottom of my heart!

To my leadership mentor, **Kim Dickson**, your support with my business and team never went unnoticed. You've motivated me when I needed it the most. Having you in my corner throughout my leadership journey has been a huge blessing. Thank you for all your support and contribution to my story.

To my friend and the Sipology founder, **Tonia Jahshan**, thank you for creating this opportunity to become a gifted leader in Sipology. Thank you for taking the risks that you did to make so many of my dreams come true. You've created one of the most positive and uplifting communities I've ever been involved in. Your authentic personality and kindness throughout my years in this company has made my experience the best it could possibly be. You are inspiring and I'm proud to share what you've created with the world.

Dracy

To our writing and editing team, thank you for helping us navigate the challenges of writing a book and...

I have many women that have played an important role in my life, that have crafted who I am and have supported me in my journey. I can't express how much support is so valuable.

First are my children, **Emily, Sinead, Conor and Casey**, my reasons why, why I have worked on my confidence, independence and worked on myself to be a better human. It was important to me to be that example and show them it was okay to make mistakes and how to learn from them and grow together. Making memories and family time has never had a price tag. I am in my highest value being able to do these things together as they have grown into the beautiful humans they are.

My mom, for being my biggest cheerleader, helped craft the kind of woman, mother and human I want to be based on her life journey. She continues to inspire me and believe anyone can change and make positive choices moving forward no matter what **hard times** you have been through. I am proud of the woman she has become.

Karen Lowen, my upline, friend, and like a sister. I learned all my getting started skills, running a business on principles skills, and annual projections from her.

She helped me create my first vision board, promoting a leader strategy, that I still use to this day and she got me reading, my first book was "Creative Visualization". She showed me the way and I will forever be grateful.

Melanie Hayden Sparks, President, Boss Lady, and business strategist. Melanie continues to play a valuable role in my life.

Never Her words of wisdom, continues to ring in my ears: "Real Impact is by leading by example."

Libby, Luella and Leigh Anne, these were the women that made me look good, I always had a PA right from my first year of leadership. They were my personal angels over the years. They did all the behind the scenes, packing, wrapping, placing orders. Everyone of them has a heart of gold, they worked relentlessly for me. I still feel I have not been able to show my gratitude for what they have done to support me. They are special and have left footprints in my heart that will last a lifetime.

Many supporters have been there for me in my journey: **George & Louise Adrian** for their continued friendship and support, **Erin Jefford** for encouraging me to write and being a great sounding board.

Cinnamon & Penny for always believing in me, and **my dad**, who has always had my back.

My mentors over the years have shaped my thinking, my character and the woman I have become today. I have studied their material, watched their seminars and immersed myself into their philosophies. **Bruce Lee, Jim Rohn, Tony Robbins, John Maxwell, Mary Christensen, Mary Kay Ash, Richard Brooke, Dan Lok** so many to name. What is important is that there are so many fantastic mentors out there to share with you.

Thank you, **Tom & Denise Chenault**, for always having a open heart and home to me and the network marketing world of misfits. And of course, writing a foreword for us.

Last, but not least, my partner in crime, **Brendon Sandford**. You truly have been worth waiting for, you continue to support me and make each day great, just by your **presence**.

About Us

Dracy Dewar

Dracy has a high level of business experience and expertise in new business, leadership, and brand development. Her network marketing career started at a young age of 23.

She has gone from a single mother on welfare to a top income earning mother of four, proving you can run a family, work from home and be the sole income earner while still living an above average lifestyle.

With a passion for connecting with people and creating an environment where relationships are forged and where people are given the opportunity to learn, grow and expand, Dracy has been able to inspire thousands by creating and supporting a sales team by helping them advance into top leadership roles. Dracy believes that the best education comes from the places you go, the people you meet and the books you read.

Leading by example, Dracy demonstrates exemplary skills in fostering relationships and engendering trust and loyalty with customers, colleagues and building dynamic teams.

Dracy's strengths include cultivating and creating space for communication, contribution & conversation. Dracy wants to help disrupt the industry in how things are done in its ever-changing landscape. She is at her highest value when she is being creative and problem-solving. Working with business builders to achieve higher results in performance, production and personal development is her aim.

Taking her last 28 years in network marketing and her passion for leadership development, she has the ability to quickly recognize and execute a plan & strategy for the desired results while creating an environment for education and experiences.

Her motto is about not just showing up, but stepping up and standing out by finding alignments between your head & heart so you can labor in a way that adds value to people's lives.

Dracy has an infectious energy that motivates & inspires those around her, whether it is the senior leaders, new business builders, or loyal customers. Her unique tools & techniques give people a willingness to make a difference and be part of something BIG.

Dracy currently lives in the Gold Coast, Qld Australia on and off for the last 20 years where she gets her daily dose of sunshine, surf and sand. Dracy enjoys being a grandmother and values her time with her family, passing on her wisdom to her growing family, that is multiplying like a network marketing business. She now consults for network marketing companies on field development and still enjoys coaching and mentoring top leaders in leadership & brand development.

Teisha Dorianna

Teisha is an ambitious Network Marketer and a passionate Social Media Strategist. Her network marketing journey began at a young age of 21 very unexpectedly. At the time,  she was a full-time university student. She had just graduated with her Bachelor's degree in Psychology and moved on to pursuing a career in elementary education. She took on the Network Marketing industry over 4 years ago as a hobby.

Teisha knew what a difference a side hustle would make from watching her hard-working mom spend her whole life working at the hospital full time and selling Avon for extra income, which helped pay for her and her brothers' sports expenses, family holidays, and extras in the family budget. Teisha was her mom's little helper growing up. She would help stamp catalogs, deliver orders, and look after hundreds of customers. Her mom would always joke around and say that she would one day become the "Avon Lady."

Teisha's oldest brother is also an entrepreneur, starting up his own successful businesses and investing in others' as well. He played a huge role in Teisha's confidence in getting started with the network marketing industry. She had all the support from her brother.

Coming from a family of entrepreneurs, Teisha got a taste of what a side hustle would do for her as a young university student.

After her first full year in the network marketing industry, she has been able to turn her hobby into her dream career through her social media platforms. She was named the #1 top recruiter and #2 personal sales in Canada in her company within her first year. After her second year, her team exploded & achieved top levels in Canada for team volume. Throughout her journey, she has gone from a shy, insecure girl to a confident woman & driven business builder. Her goal is to help ambitious network marketers create residual income through social media and a network marketing platform.

One of Teisha's strengths is to take a topic and find multiple ways to teach and train by maximizing the platforms and tools available to her. Being a Millennial on the border of a Gen Z, she was born into a world of peak technological innovation — where information was immediately accessible and social media increasingly ubiquitous. She has been able to deliver a new feel and flavor to the industry by growing a network marketing business and community completely online. Teisha is financially minded and gives people a sense of security by being conservative with a future focused vision of growth, development, and unlimited opportunities.

Being an entrepreneur is an expression of her values and identity, crafting her brand to be innovative and creative. Her focus is about being brave and just doing it anyway. She will always keep it real, raw, authentic, and fun in everything she does. As Teisha would say, "If it makes you happy, it doesn't have to make sense to anyone else."

She is a mental health advocate and makes a mountain look like a mole hill with a party at the top, by delivering practical steps, appropriate tools and loads of encouragement. You are never alone when you are working with Teisha.

Her high school sweetheart and partner Ryan resides just outside Edmonton, Alberta, Canada with their most recent addition, a cat named Earl. He is named after Teisha's favorite tea, Earl Grey. Together, Teisha and Ryan have recently purchased their first home and they're loving their new beginning.

Leave a Review on Amazon

Thank you for making it to the end of our book. Please take 60 seconds to leave us a review for "The Unwrapped Leader" on Amazon. Tell us what you thought of our book! You will be glad you did.

Made in the USA
Las Vegas, NV
12 October 2024